I Used to be Normal, Then I Got Bored

Trusting There's More...

Arael

Wild Flower Press
P.O. Box 1429
Columbus, NC 28722

Library of Congress Cataloging-in-Publication Data

Arael, Nancy, 1947-
I used to be normal, but then I got bored : trusting there's more / Arael.
    pages cm
Includes bibliographical references.
ISBN 978-0-926524-48-4
1. Arael, Nancy, 1947- 2. Women healers--United States--Biography.
3. Women shamans--United States--Biography. 4. Spiritualists
--United States--
Biography. I. Title.
RZ408.A696A3 2014
615.8'52--dc23

                              2014041836

Manuscript Editor: Brian L. Crissey & Pamela Meyer
Manuscript & Cover Designer: Pamela Meyer
Cover Vision: Arael

Printed in the United States of America.

Address all inquiries to:
Wild Flower Press, an imprint of Granite Publishing
P.O. Box 1429
Columbus, NC 28722
http://granite-planet.net

Dedication

I wish to thank all the men, women and animals

in my physical and spiritual families

for their love and support.

About the Cover

Everything in a dream is a symbol that represents a part of you. The cover was inspired by a dream I had.

The *horse* is the symbol for *power,* and the *white horse* represents *wisdom in power*—those who are willing to carry responsibility in a balanced manner.

The *cliff* represents coming to the edge of "All that you Know," to a *place* where you need to take a Leap of Faith into the Unknown. There is an anonymous quote that goes "When you come to the edge of all that you know, you are given one of two things, land to stand on or Wings to Fly."

On the *cliff* is the Rune symbol M which represents *movement, progress*—the *horse* can also symbolize a place of transition and movement; of physical shifts, new dwelling places, new attitudes or new life. It also signifies movement in the sense of improving or bettering any situation.

The *horse* signifies the bond between horse and rider that enables you to feel a measure of safety in your position. It represents a time to turn again and face the future reassured.

Finally, the *rainbow* represents the connection, or the bridge between, Heaven and Earth.

Table of Contents

Preface

I did not intend to write a book at any time in my life, but I kept getting messages from my spiritual side that I needed to do so. When I finally surrendered to Spirit and said, "OK, I give up—tell me what I need to do, and I will write." That is when Spirit—in its great sense of humor—took charge! The signs began appearing to me one after another.

One day one of those signs came in the form of an older woman who came in for a reading at the shop where I worked. She had a cane, huge white hair, and a small, thin body. I asked if I could be of assistance to her, and she immediately snapped that if she wanted my help, she would ask for it! I smiled and left her alone. After about 20 minutes, as she was looking around the store, she approached me and asked for a reading—but just a short one. After leading her to my table, I asked for permission to work with her Higher Self and Spirit Guides. I then asked for what I needed to see for her happiness and growth. What I saw through the reading was a book. I conveyed some of the other things that came to me, and I finally had to ask her, "Are you writing a book or wanting to write a book?"

She looked surprised, and then she shared that she had been told for many years to write a book, but she never thought of herself as a writer. "I'm 89 years old, and do I even have enough time to write this book?"

I let her know that she was going to be around for a while and that she needed to begin the book and just write, and it would come to her. She thanked me, got her cane and left.

As she was leaving, it dawned on me that I was saying the very same thing that she was, and I realized that I had just given myself a reading as well! I would be her in 40 years if I didn't start to write. I laughed and began thinking about this book in earnest.

Like any writer, my first thought was, "Where do I begin?" I then got an email from my nephew informing me of a dream he had about me and a man whom I would meet who writes screenplays. In the next couple of days that dream came true when I met Michael, my mentor. He came into the shop with his partner, who wanted a reading from another woman. As Michael was waiting for his partner, we talked. During our conversation, he mentioned that he had helped his partner write a screenplay. Suddenly my nephew's dream popped into my head, and I told Michael about the older woman who had come in several days before and how I was being led to write a book. Michael was very sweet in explaining to me how I should begin. As they were leaving, he handed me his card, saying "Call me when you write your first chapter." Knowing that I had someone to call on gave me the courage to start.

Later that night I asked for a title to my book, and the name I received as Annieville.

To me, "Annieville" made sense, because it represented my conception of what I helped to create in my life. My first name, Nancy (named after my father's Aunt in France) means gracious, and comes from Anne, which also means grace. These aspects around grace became clearer to me even more so when, later in my life, I found out that my heart totem is the Swan, which means graceful. Since the abuse in our family began on my Mother Anne's side of the family, I could see why "Annieville" came to mind. When I got introduced to my heart totem, I realized that my transformation from abused child (ugly duckling) to graceful swan (full of grace) was, and is, my journey in this lifetime. And my sharing this transition is the real purpose of this book.

I also researched the women in my Dad's family, and I found out that seven generations before, the women had to go underground to escape persecution from the leaders of the Catholic church. They were wise women who shared their healing gifts, but they were called heretics, among other names. During a time in my life when I was doing some deep meditation, I received a disturbing vision, which I'll share later, of an abused woman. I was told then that "I would fix it in time." While doing this research and combining it with my own life history of abuse, I realized what my soul already knew—I had to experience the childhood that I did so I could heal the experience from the inside out, which would also heal generations of women before and after me. By walking this particular *physical* path, I was given the foundation for my *spiritual* path.

Just because "Annieville" meant so much to me didn't mean that its meaning would be obvious to someone picking up this book. So, the title has changed, as you can see, because this book, as I am, are works in progress. But then again, I may have been given that "name" because of how it related to the contents of the book, not just the title.

My purpose in writing this book is to share pieces of my life story through my stories, thereby letting people know of possibilities they may never have even imagined. Over the years, when helping other people, a particular story would always pop up in my head, which I would relay. Always, the person receiving it would say, "That's exactly what I needed to hear." When I asked the question to Spirit as to what I should write about, the stories were made clear to me for each chapter, and so I wrote.

I desire to help others find out who they really are. It was not an easy journey for me to take, but I am glad I did.

It was not easy growing from an abused child into a woman who knows she is loved, even when the ones around her are not showing her love, but since I overcame so much, I intend to help others, no matter what their situation. Most women around the world have self-esteem issues, whether they've been abused or not. I hope to help readers truly to love themselves, whether they are alone, with others who love them, or currently with those who do not. I hope to convey how living in the moment without fearing the future or regretting the past can bring one deep peace. I will share how I moved from learning my lessons through pain and grief, to learning them through love and laughter.

In my early life, I had difficulty trusting anyone at all, and now I live completely on trust. I originally had little courage to accomplish anything, and yet now I live what I dream. I'm certainly not the only one who can do this. We all can, and I hope this book helps you begin to live what you dream.

1... Harvest

Rune symbol for Harvest
This symbol has beneficial outcomes, it applies
to any activity or endeavor to which you are
committed.

I remember when I first thought about meeting Liza—an intuitive artist. I listened to a tape she made in which she was channeling angelic beings. I liked her voice, but most of all I loved her sense of humor about it all. My real desire was to have her do a drawing of my Higher Self and a reading to interpret the symbols in the portrait. However, meeting this person would not be easy, since she lived over 2,000 miles away. So I never thought I would ever have the opportunity to do so. Then one day my friend Paula told me that in a month Liza would be at a conference on the East coast to give a weekend workshop. Paula, who held meditation groups at her house, sometimes played tapes on spiritual subjects, and Liza's tapes had been some of my favorites. Even though it was the East coast, it would still be a 14-hour drive. To have the experience of a weekend with this joyous woman, however, would be worth the drive. I was thrilled, to say the least—finally I would get to meet Liza in person.

On our way there, we talked about what it might be like to be at the workshop site and experience Black Mountain, North

Carolina. Paula had been there many times before, and she told me
how beautiful the little town was and how it was surrounded by
hills covered with lush forests. I also just love to travel and
experience new vistas with the sun rising and setting on different
horizons. Some people get tired of traveling, but it seems to give me
new perspectives for life.

When we arrived, I wasn't disappointed. Black Mountain truly is
nestled in the Blue Ridge Mountains, and it is quite beautiful. It is an
artsy town with lots of quaint stores and houses that you can tell
were owned by very creative people who weren't afraid to express
their creativity to produce unique surroundings.

Since we registered too late to get rooms at the conference, we
decided to arrive the day before the workshop to find a place to stay
nearby so we didn't have to rush to and from the workshop every
morning. This way we could truly enjoy the peace, quiet and beauty
of the area. Our first preference was a quaint bed and breakfast. We
didn't make reservations ahead of time, because Paula had been
there before and was sure that there would be no problem in
finding a place that would suit us. Little did we know that every year
at that time, Black Mountain holds its annual arts festival that brings
people from "miles around." To say the least, we were about to see a
preview of what other amazing events would occur during the
weekend that would test our trust in the powers that be.

We drove around the town several times without finding a place
to rest our tired bodies. Paula was driving, becoming more tired and
irritated by the minute, and it didn't help her mood any when I
asked,

"Why don't we just manifest something that will fit our needs?"

"This is not the time to be spiritual. We have to be practical," she
replied.

I didn't quite understand this, because I felt that it was the perfect time to put this particular skill into action. We were not only being given a golden opportunity, but we were really in need of a place to stay.

If there is one thing I have learned along the way though, it is that if people in your space do not want to hear something you have to say, they will clearly show you by their actions. And Paula was doing that, so I kept quiet. Then I had a brainstorm!

"Why don't you let me drive, so you can rest?" I asked her.

At first, she hesitated, but then she gave into her weariness. Once I got behind the wheel, I closed my eyes and asked the Universe to lead us to a place to rest for the weekend that would be clean and reasonably priced.

I started the car and let guidance prevail. I drove awhile, when the wheel of her vehicle literally started pulling towards the left. I turned into the next street and drove a little ways to a bed and breakfast on my left.

Paula perked up and said, "I never realized that there was a B&B on this street."

I parked in front, and we both jumped out and headed for the lobby. Paula asked the woman behind the desk, if by chance there might be one or two rooms available for us.

The woman replied apologetically, "I am afraid not. Everything we have is booked for the entire weekend."

At this point, Paula turned to look at me, as if to say, "What do you make of this?"

I then felt compelled to ask the woman if she knew of anything even in the surrounding areas where we could find accommodations! She frowned, but then her face lit up!

"Wait a minute," she said, "sometimes the nearby Christian Retreat Center rents rooms if they've had cancellations for their own programs."

She called and was informed that they happened to have two cancellations just an hour before. The price was unbelievably low—$30.00 per night per person. We got directions and jumped back into the car. As we drove in, we realized that our weekend was going to be spent in a beautiful place by a gorgeous stream, surrounded by tall green trees, with walking paths leading into the surrounding forests. This retreat center was not only exactly what we needed, but it was also located very close to our workshop Thank you, Universe! Paula had faith once again, and we both agreed that this was a sign of what we had in store for the weekend.

Once we settled into our rooms, we headed to dinner, taking this time to sit, relax and receive good nourishment. After dinner we were revived and ready to head for the workshop site to register and to meet our teacher and the other participants. The workshop was held at a hilltop retreat center, overlooking a beautiful valley with green trees everywhere.

As we entered the meeting room, there was Liza, sitting with a few women around her. When she saw us enter, she rose to greet us. She was tall and thin, with light brown hair, almost golden brown. Her hair was chin length, and she was wearing a flowing pastel-colored ankle-length dress. She smiled as she came toward us. She reached out to give me a hug and I reached to receive her, all the while feeling a little shy and humbled by her openness.

As we hugged, she whispered in my ear, "It is so good to see you again!"

"Yeah, me too," I quickly blurted out, but actually I was stunned and speechless, to say the least. Being a little shaken by this, yet excitedly pleased at the same time, I got myself seated.

The entire weekend was memorable for us. We both had a few enlightened moments, and we enjoyed long discussions every evening about what we had felt and learned from each day's events. However, for each one us, the main event was the private session with Liza in which she would draw our Higher Selves, explaining what she was receiving while she drew. We knew beforehand that we could record the sessions, so we came fully prepared with some tapes.

Our appointments were the last two of the day, with Paula's being last. As the women before us came out of their private sessions, they willingly showed us their portraits and told us what they received in their readings. My anticipation continued to grow, until my turn came, and she came out to greet me. Once again she acknowledged that we knew each other. I did have a feeling of warmth and affection for her, and I wondered why. How and where did we know each other? It definitely wasn't this lifetime, because I would have remembered! So, I asked her how we knew each other, and she said, "You'll remember, just give it some time."

"OK", I said.

"Did you bring a tape to record the session?" she asked.

"Yes," I responded, giving her the tape.

"Do you have any questions before we proceed?" she gently asked.

"No, maybe afterwards," I said, since I couldn't think of anything off hand.

She then described to me a little of what to expect while in session. She explained that she goes into a trance state but is still able to draw. Once the information begins to come, the drawing just flows through her, and with a pencil in her hand, she draws whatever comes out. When the drawing is complete, she views it, prays for guidance, and then explains what it all means.

When she came out of her trance, she looked at what she drew and showed it to me. It was amazing to see something so well done and precise. While she was drawing I was watching her, and it looked to me as if she had her eyes almost shut while drawing the portrait of my Higher Self. It was very beautiful, and I wished that I truly looked as pretty as her drawing. I never really thought of myself as beautiful, or even pretty, but then I was thinking, "Well, at least I look pretty good on a higher level!"

Then her face changed dramatically, and she said, "Oh, my! I never really dreamed that it was like this! I have to change what I was taught and change my mind about how it all happened! Do you see what I drew around the top of your head—this brilliance of light shooting out in all directions, with stars inside of the brilliance?"

"Yes," I said.

"You're a genius," she gasped. "Not only that, but a genius from a distant galaxy in a different universe!"

"What?" I exclaimed. Now I was very sure that she had the wrong person! I was good in science and math in school, but a genius?

"Well, I would say I was an average student, but no way near genius quality!", I blurted out. "And from another galaxy and different universe? Do other universes even exist?"

Then I remembered how much I loved science fiction as a child, and how I would gaze up at the stars, praying to God that I wanted to go home, and how I wished I had my own spaceship to fly me there. But don't all kids do that?

"Well," Liza interrupted my thought process. "I don't exactly mean genius in the limited sense in which it is used today. We get so stuck with our limited vocabulary in talking about the vast universe. Did you know that the original Latin verb was *genui*, which referred to bringing something into being, or creating or producing something? What I'm seeing here relates to the word in that way."

I was still flabbergasted, but Liza went on. She said that her vision showed that the call went out to all the geniuses (or creators) from different galaxies and universes to create something new and different. A handful of these geniuses showed up here, and I was one of them. We brought together our brilliance to create something never created before.

"No way!" I exclaimed. But then I wondered why am I not leaving? Why am I still sitting here, wanting more? Well, I had to admit that this story was too fascinating to just leave. I wanted to see where she would go from here, and why was this about me? I knew that she hadn't said this kind of thing to the previous women, because they had told different stories.

She continued to say that the handful of geniuses that showed up brought with them their own stories of their unique creations from their various universes and by combining these experiences, this new creation was formed. Their energies and wisdom helped to visualize a new concept—a new place to *be*.

In her vision, she saw me over Africa, creating trees and leaves from the palms of my hands. She saw beautiful birds and leopards flying out of my hair and other four-leggeds coming out of the lining of my coat. Since there was such a wondrous commotion throughout space, other beings came to watch. She envisioned them watching from huge spaceships, just enjoying the show. Then, once it was all done, these creators felt tremendous love for their new creation, and the watching space beings wanted to take things from this beautiful site and re-create it in their own galaxies.

All of a sudden, what she was revealing to me became a vision in my own mind. It was hard to watch. I was just wishing it would stay in its purity awhile longer, and then I realized that all of creation needed to be shared. The watchers started to take and take. It was almost like watching a young and beautiful virgin being horribly raped.

At that moment, I began to deeply sob, from the depths of my soul! I blurted out, "Why couldn't they just leave it all alone, without trying to manipulate and then destroy it for their own gains?"

I looked at her while I was saying this, and I could not believe that these words were coming from my mouth. Did I really see this from my soul memories? Was I really there? How could this be? Why is this happening, and why do I feel so sad—like a mother helplessly watching her child being destroyed, unable to do anything about it? I wanted this to stop, but Liza went on.

"These are energies to show you that you are protected on all levels." She pointed out some energy swirls on different levels in the drawing.

Now I knew that she was joking! As a child, I had been badly beaten to the point that my left leg got broken. Where was my protection then?

I don't remember what she said next. All I knew was that when this session was done, I planned to listen to the tape again, to see if what I heard was correct, and then maybe all of this would make some sense.

We hugged, and I thanked her, but as I was a bit dazed and felt weak, I could not say much more. I took the portrait and tape with me. Paula was waiting outside, looking forward to her turn.

"How was it?" asked Paula.

I just smiled and said, "Good, I think." I told her that I would fill her in later, after her own session.

I was glad that most of the women had gone already, so I could just sit there with my eyes closed and rest, waiting for Paula. What Liza told me was so sensational that I was still having difficulty with it sinking in.

When Paula came out of her session, she wanted to talk, but I asked her to wait until later, which she agreed to do.

With a long drive ahead of us, we got on the road right away to put some miles behind us. When we stopped for a late lunch, Paula asked about my session and what was said. I told her to go first. She was happy to tell me her story and all that was given to her. I found myself wondering what I could say to her when it was my time to share my session. We both felt that her story felt true, but it wasn't as "out there" as mine.

Then she said, "Tell me yours."

At first I said, I do not know whether or not to believe what she told me, and I was embarrassed to relay any of it. Then I thought to myself, why not tell her? She will say it is a whole lot of BS, and then I can agree and forget about all of it. So I blurted it all out and waited for Paula to say that it truly was all BS.

Paula looked at me, saying, "I believe it."

"What? You believe that I could be one of these geniuses that helped create this world?"

"Yes," she said, looking me right in the eyes.

"You are telling me that you honestly believe that this could be true?"

"Yes. I've always known that you were more than amazing. When we talk each week at our meditation group, you always have stories about manifesting all kinds of things, instantly and easily. You have things happening to you on a daily basis that most of us only dream would happen, and your dreams come true."

I could not believe my ears. Paula, of all people, was always cutting me off and putting me down by making the stories and adventures I had to tell each week seem less than important. I did not expect that she would ever be saying such things.

After our animated discussion, the trip home seemed long and silent. At times, Paula was her old self—criticizing me—but never about the story I told her about my session with Liza.

When I finally got home, I made a bee-line for my tape recorder. I wanted to hear this whole story again, with new ears. But when I turned on the recorder, there was nothing but static for the entire tape! It had not recorded! I was so upset that I called Paula to see if her tape had recorded. She said that she put her tape on as soon as she got home as well, and her tape was loud and clear. How was this possible? I went before her!

I never did get the larger portrait that I had paid for, but only the smaller sketch that Liza did in our session. I often wondered why Liza kept the larger portrait, even after numerous phone calls. She always said that she needed more time to finish it. Maybe she never finished it, or maybe because I never believed what she said, I wasn't allowed to receive it? I may never know.

I continued my meditation groups, and I tried to forget what Liza had told me. Every once in a while, I remember that reading and wonder about it, but I could not ever really know the truth. I've seen too many people claim that they were some kind of Master or another and lose sight of reality. I have a life—sometimes good and sometimes not so good—but good enough. At that time in my life, I loved working at the high school, counseling young adults, and raising my baby boy. To me, that was what was important!

This chapter was not easy to write. I wrote it first only because it was the one that first popped into my mind. I believe that maybe since I had such low self-esteem for so long, and believed I was not much and not worthy of much, Spirit decided to get my attention. Maybe that is why I was given this "vision" from Liza, so I could do more with my life, and not settle for "good enough." Maybe they felt I would be shocked into believing that maybe I was more? Whether or not what I heard from Liza was true, or not, it worked. I did begin believing in myself more.

Sometimes we all need a jolt like this—to see a vision of our higher selves—to realize that each of us is truly powerful at a higher level. Our society does not support this kind of outlook, and, unfortunately, as children we are too often demeaned, spending our whole lifetimes trying to rise up out of the ashes. I know I did.

2... Ribbons

If I dream of ribbons or having a ribbon on me or wrapped around something, it usually relates to the power to bind or loosen something. In other connections it may also be an image of bonds.

My nephew Christopher has survived family ordeals beyond his rocky start in this world, which was an ordeal in itself. When my sister went into a coma during his birth, his first experience was being pulled by forceps into the outside world. The doctors told us that he might not live, which was understandable: Who would want to be forced into the world when you're not quite ready for it? His next immediate trauma is that he lost his mother.

I did have premonitions about my sister's death, but as I was only a kid myself, I couldn't tell anyone and be accepted for it. When children speak of such things, too often they hear that is just their imagination. Do we receive these premonitions to prepare for traumatic events coming our way? I think so. Had my family been open to such things, maybe my sister's death would have been handled better.

Due to the fact that my family did not handle my sister's death well, I was not able to really know my nephew until he was a teenager. I knew that my mother needed help, and I suggested to one of my aunts that she get counseling. Even I knew at my young age that my sister's death was creating mental instability in my mother., but going to a counselor in those days was not readily accepted. So, my mother carried on with unresolved feelings causing more issues.

I remember when Chris's father came to my parents' door. I knew it was coming. He had told my parents that he was concerned about the effect on his son of all the drama created by my mother, who did not get along his new wife. He wanted a new start, and he told my mother, "As far as you are concerned, in Chris's life, you are dead." That was my mother's drama, and my dad went along with it, as he always did to keep the peace. I was angry at both sides, because all I knew was that I would never see Christopher again. To me, the reason was that the so-called adults were playing out their dramas and saying that they were doing the best for Christopher, but really they were only serving themselves.

Over the years, I explained to my mother that I understood how she created unnecessary drama in her life, and how all the created drama made her life unhappy. Sometimes I thought I saw a light in her eyes that she "got" what I had said to her, but as soon as the light came on, she would put it out by saying, "I don't know what you are talking about. I have done my duty, and I know that I have a place in Heaven when I die!"

How sad, I would think, that she believed that the whole purpose of life was to do your duty, even if it makes you unhappy, then offer your grief up to God to ensure yourself a better place in Heaven when you die.

It was only after I was older, married, and out of my parents' house that I decided to try to see Christopher again. It wasn't easy at first—we were total strangers—but I wasn't about to give up on our relationship. After all, he is my sister's son, and nothing will ever change that, for which I am glad! Now Chris lives in New York City with his partner Trey and has created a great life for himself!

I bless my mother for all she has given me, which has shown me and given me even more courage to live the life I was meant to live—from my heart! Even more than that—through all the dramas, I have learned another sense of purpose. By living through these experiences, I have gained the wisdom to help others get through their own dramas, whether created by them or those around them.

3... Protection

Rune symbol for Protection
Control of the emotions is the issue here...remain
mindful that timely right action is your true
protection.

Young people can be driven crazy, at times, between the
pressures of growing up, adults seeming not to hear them, and
their trying to be what they perceive as being cool or popular. In
my teenage years, not only did I feel this way, but I also had
Catholic School pressures about which actions God and the nuns
would perceive as sins that needed punishment. In my sophomore
year, a nun who was my counselor asked me what I would
consider to be a good career for myself. I happened to be very
good in science and math—I loved analyzing things and coming
up with the answers, so my answer was, "Since I am so good in
science and math and love doing laboratory work, Sister, maybe
something in that field?"

Her answer to me was, "Well, you can be a teacher, a nurse or
maybe a medical secretary."

I was shocked, and I answered her, "But, Sister, what if I don't
want to be any of those things?"

She answered, as she patted me on the arm, "Well, my dear,
you could always be a housewife."

I could not believe my ears! Those were my only choices? Well, we would just see about that!

I have a fond memory of the day I graduated from that school. I went to the back of my yard, where my mother often burned trash in a big barrel. I took my catholic uniform and books and smiled as they all went up in smoke! Later, when I chose to became a career counselor, I swore to myself that I would never limit anyone else in their choices.

One day after several years on this job, I met a young woman named Denise. The first time I met her, she was assisted into my office by a teacher's aide. Not only did Denise have cerebral palsy, but she was also legally blind. She told me that she could only see light, nothing else. Unfortunately, she was put into an incubator with too much oxygen, which affected her optic nerve and the part of her brain that controls proper coordination and muscular functions. She had been mainstreamed into a huge population of normal students who mostly were physically fit, normal teenagers.

I had been counseling for a few years when she came into my office, but it was the first time that I felt a little scared, and I wondered what I could possibly do to help her with her career choices? However, as I got to know her over the next three years, we became friends, and I discovered what she could teach me.

I became accustomed to her saying things like, "See you later, and did you see that TV show last night?"

Initially I was surprised by such statements, and I would ask her, "Denise, how can you see a TV show?"

She explained that by using her senses of hearing and feeling, she would inwardly see what was going on, and then, when the scenes became very quiet, she would just ask her Mom to fill in the blanks.

One day, she told me about a dream she had the night before. She began to describe the colors of certain things in her dreams. Again, I asked, "Denise, how do you see colors?"

"I feel them. I feel the color blue and it makes me feel cool, then I feel red and it makes me feel warm."

This is when I began to realize that most of our senses are under utilized. Sight and hearing, while wonderful—I definitely don't want to give them up—may just limit us in other ways.

I am truly grateful to have had teachers like Denise throughout my life to help me to become aware of hidden aspects of myself. She, by the way, graduated with high honors and went on to earn higher degrees in several areas.

After Denise got me started, I began to train myself to focus more on a given sound or a certain scent in the room, and it would take on a new element. Then I started to concentrate on the feeling I would get when someone or something was approaching me. This process of focusing on my environment kept increasing my intuitive senses, which we don't normally use. This greater sensitivity helped me to respond to situations, rather than to react to them.

Humans are not the only super-sensitive beings. I once read that elephants, for example, have poor eyesight, but they are extremely responsive to the sounds, rather than the visual movements, around them. They also have a tremendous sense of smell, and when they breathe in, they envision their environment. They also can feel and remember if someone has hurt them or has treated them well, which is probably like a dog that can spend five minutes smelling your clothing, tires and car to see where you have been, who you were with, and what you ate while away. In *The Secret Life of Plants*, polygraph machines proved that plants are highly tuned into the humans who care for them, their moods and feelings. They could also sense if someone had an intent to hurt them when a person walked into the room.

By staying calm, listening, observing and feeling what is going on around us, we can learn to respond fully and sensitively to what is happening around us.

Learning to use all my senses as a high school counselor was very beneficial. Teenagers don't speak very much, and they have a hard time trusting adults. With my new found sensitivity, I could feel when they would emphasize certain words. I could feel when they weren't breathing, and I could more readily sense their anxieties. Sometimes, I could actually feel their pain, but one has to keep that under control so as to be clear for the person you are counseling. I learned to respond by listening more and speaking less and being more caring and compassionate. It is funny that as a child, I was told that I was being too sensitive! In that job, my sensitivity was valuable, and it continues to be so.

On top of being "overly sensitive," according to some, I also had the ability since I was a little girl; to see what others could not see. I always thought it was normal, until I tried to speak to people around me about what I was seeing, and I was told to stop being so different. I was told to see and think like everyone else. I also had prophetic dreams that would come true, but whenever I told someone about these, I was criticized.

It was while I was a counselor that my third eye became more developed. I always had a keen eye for observation, but further development would give me flashes of sight (vivid pictures) of some scene that was relevant for the student standing in front of me. I then would casually say something about what I felt and saw, which sometimes would bring on conversations that led to deeper levels of understanding so I could better comprehend where the student was coming from and where I should go with it.

I was never much for placing or even reading statements on tee-shirts, but I must say that there was an event that I was glad to have experienced during my high school years. I call it my "Tee-Shirt Wisdom" event.

One day, one of my co-counselors walked into my room and showed me an advertisement in the back of a magazine that read, "You too can be a 'Hug Therapist' and let the world know it by buying a tee-shirt in said ad, available in three different colors and various sizes. The tee-shirt read "Hug Therapist" across the top with a huggy bear beneath it.

She approached me with the idea that we should purchase one for her and one for me in different colors, and we could wear them to work one day. I was amazed that she suggested such an idea, for in my mind, we were professionals, and wearing something that casual on our jobs was being very unprofessional!

She persisted, and after considerable consideration, we both agreed that it would be fun to just wear them on an in-service day where students were only in school for half a day.

I completely forgot about ordering the tee-shirts, and then one day she walked into my room, held up a tee-shirt and said, "Aren't they great? And they arrived just in time so we can wear them next in-service day."

I was taken aback since the next in-service day just happened to be the following Friday. At this point in time, I still did not think it was such a good idea, but I agreed to wear mine for the half day of school.

When Friday came, the other counselor really enjoyed giving hugs to everyone in sight, but, I stayed in my office, in the hopes that no one would come in. But, as the day progressed, many of the students, secretaries, and teachers alike came in looking for their hug. I began to thoroughly enjoy that I was wearing the "Hug Therapist" tee-shirt, and towards the end of the morning when the students were about to leave, one particular young man was standing in my doorway, neither in nor out. I instantly recognized him, and I asked, "Craig, how can I be of help to you, today?"

He hesitated; he looked down and then looked up and said, "I understand that you are giving hugs today?"

It surprised me, for he had never shown any emotion before when I had worked with him. In the past he would just get his information and leave, sometimes without even a "Thank you." I went over to him, gave him his hug, which he openly received, and I sadly realized that this was the first time in two and a half years that I saw him smile.

I've come to realize how important it is not to judge how wisdom comes to us—just be open to receive it, even if it's on a tee-shirt. How does one be open and receive? Try not to think and talk ourselves into believing our thoughts are the only true thoughts. You just might learn something great!

4...   The Broken Watch

In a dream a watch obviously means "it's about time," and for it to be broken, it can represent that "in time, something needs to be fixed!"

After many years of counseling people, I learned that pets often reflect what their owners need to look at within themselves. So, when my dog died of liver problems several years ago, I knew somehow that he was telling me that my health was in jeopardy. I had been having some pain in both the liver and the spleen, so I decided to begin caring for myself. Luckily, I was at a place in life where I could take a couple of months off to heal my liver and spleen problems. Western medicine is good at working with symptoms, but most other healing methodologies around the world believe that the illness begins in the emotional and spirit side first, and then it manifests physically. So, I knew it would be important for me to look deeply within.

Several times a day I meditated, focusing on what I needed to do in order to heal. During one of my deep meditations, I saw a disturbing vision of a woman being murdered by her husband and two brothers. I witnessed the men in a dirt basement of a small house, covering a wooden casket. After they nailed the casket cover shut, they began talking about how they had forgotten to place some of her belongings inside the casket, and whether or not they should reopen it to do that. Neither one wanted to reopen the casket, so they came up with the idea of making a small box on top in which to place her things. They then placed the casket in a hole they had dug in this basement.

As I watched this scene, I wondered why I was witnessing this horrible event. I was told to continue watching, and it would be revealed to me later.

In the vision, I emerged from the basement and saw that I was in a small European village. As I stood in the street, I looked down and saw a broken watch with a mother-of-pearl face. Rose quartz and moonstone beads made up the band, and, for some reason, I knew this watch belonged to the murdered woman. At the same time, I also knew that the village was from many generations before my lifetime, and that the watch would not have existed during that time period. I was told to take the watch, and I would "fix it in time."

When I came out of the vision, I asked, "Why was I shown this vision, and who were those people?" I was then told that these people were in my lineage, as far back as six generations.

I asked, "Was I her, or anyone else, in the vision?"

"No."

I was told that this vision was given to me so I could learn that the purpose for being a woman in this lifetime and choosing the abusive family that I did was in order to help heal many generations. So I understood clearly that my lifetime of going through the abuse I had experienced firsthand, while growing up in my family, was so I could truly know and experience what I had come here to heal.

"Is that why I was told when I picked up her watch, that I would fix it in time?"

"Yes."

I also asked, "Did the mother-of-pearl face with rose quartz and moonstone beads that made up the band have a meaning?"

"The watch represented her, in her lifetime. She was considered to be a wonderful mother. She loved her children and those around her, and she was very giving, especially with her insights."

They went on to explain further that she met her future husband when he came into her village with his two brothers, looking for a wife. He was very handsome and much older than she was. He romanced her and swept her off her feet. After the marriage ceremony, his true colors emerged, and he became very abusive. She stayed with him, bearing him two children because, in her religion, it was important to honor her vows.

Once he started to abuse the children, however, she planned her escape. Unfortunately, the brothers discovered her plan and came up with one of their own: They decided to tell everyone that she ran off with a traveler who had come through the village, which was why forgetting to put her things in the coffin was a problem, because they wanted to show that she only took what she could carry and what was precious to her. When none of the brothers could come up with a better plan, they decided to bury all of her belongings. The people of the village did not believe their story, but since they couldn't disprove it either, they had no other choice but to accept it.

After this vision, it became quite clear why I chose to become human and a woman in this life, and why I experienced the childhood that I did.

By experiencing abuse myself and seeing the result of that kind of behavior, I have been able to stop further abuse in my family by never abusing or hurting anyone in any way or accepting abuse from anyone in anyway.

We often do not realize that we all have this kind of power to change the lives of our descendants, but we do. Additionally, when we change behaviors in this life, we can also heal those who came before us.

5... Fertility/New

Rune symbol for Fertility
Control of the emotions is the issue here...remain
mindful that timely right action is your true
protection.

I was young; I had a beautiful house, a wonderful child and a great job that I loved—everything that most people believe should give them happiness. But I felt restless, with a void inside that I seemed unable to fill. Because I should have been happy, I kept wondering—what was wrong with me?

I decided to light a fire in the fireplace one night while listening to some music and enjoying an evening alone. My son was sleeping overnight at my parents' house, and my then-husband was away, golfing with his guy friends. I put on one of my favorite albums, "The Dark Side of The Moon" by Pink Floyd.

The song "Time" came on. I was deep into thinking that my life was meaningless, and I felt like I was wasting time! Bored and miserable, I started to cry and scream out to God, "I know I am not doing what I came here to do, but I don't know what that is. I am wasting time, so show me what it is, or just please take me!"

I truly felt that the world and my son would be better off without me. I knew that this void inside had better be filled, or I would end up feeling worse, and who wants to be around someone who feels empty and sad?

I also knew that I would not commit suicide—what a mess that would be to clean up! I knew that God had the power to just lift me out of this body and that He would easily replace me with someone better to take my place.

Screaming to God felt pretty good! I never allowed myself to do that before.

All of a sudden, I had a brief memory of standing at the foot of a hospital bed, six years earlier. My older sister was in a coma; they told us that she had experienced a cerebral hemorrhage. She had just given birth to a baby boy, but they weren't sure he would live. The birth did not cause my sister's coma—it could have happened at any other time in her life. I knew that if she died, my life would become a living hell. I asked God at that time to please let my sister live and for me to be taken in her place. I quickly changed my mind then, because I was not ready to die.

But this time I felt that I was ready to go.

After that brief moment of remembering the last time I wanted to leave my body, due to my sister's death, I continued to scream, and once again I told God to take me: "I am wasting time here on Earth!"

All of a sudden, I felt a peace come over me, with a calming sense of bliss that I had never felt before. I opened my eyes, and there, in the middle of my living room, was a huge dark wooden door. It took up a space that was as big as the fireplace that went all the way up to the cathedral ceiling, and there was light coming out around all the edges of the door. I walked over to the door and opened it. I felt the doorknob in my hand. The light was brilliant, and I saw a vastness of light and space. I wanted to walk into it, but I saw that there was nothing to support me. I asked for support so I could walk into the light. Clouds began to form. I then walked on the clouds into the space of light. This was pure bliss! I was being supported by clouds.

"Wait a minute! How can this be?", I screamed. "What could these clouds be made of to support me?"

A voice came out of the light, saying, "Wasted time? Wasted time? What does that mean?"

The vision disappeared, and again I was standing in my living room. I was wide awake. I had no alcohol or drugs (never did drugs) in my system. I knew something just happened that I could not explain away. I was left feeling at peace, God had heard me, but what did this all mean? Wasted time?

I had a peaceful sleep that night with no dreams to speak of, so I awakened the next morning happily singing to myself. I had to pick up my son at my parents' house, but first I had to go grocery shopping.

This sense of peace stayed with me. As I was walking through the supermarket, a woman approached me and called my name. She looked a little familiar to me, and once we spoke, she reminded me that we had a mutual woman friend. She told me that she was excited about the new metaphysical bookstore that opened on Route 61.

At that time in my life I was pretty clueless about spiritual matters and asked, "What is metaphysical?"

"You know—spiritual books on reincarnation and stuff."

I never heard the word before but I did have a curiosity about reincarnation. Then and there I made a mental note to visit this store in the near future. I had always felt that there was more to life than I had been taught and my vision left me wanting more. From that point on, I vowed to continue opening the door to my own enlightenment.

I still did not know what the voice meant by telling me that the clouds were made from "wasted time." This confusion helped me to heed the search.

When I did visit the metaphysical book store, I bought several books and became a sponge for more spiritual knowledge. With each book, my life made more sense—the dreams that came true, the visions of past lives, the desires and restlessness of wanting more. I thought I needed more money or material things, and all along, it was more fulfillment of my spirit that I needed. I was beginning to fill the void inside, not outside!

On my continued search for enlightenment, I let go of finding out what "wasted time" meant, which was when I found it. I was planning a long weekend away to a small Caribbean Island. Living in the Northeast with its long winters gets to be very depressing by the middle of February. I found a couple of cheap airline tickets and a very reasonable hotel for my husband and me. I decided to stop by the metaphysical bookstore for something to read on the trip.

I wanted something easy to read, yet spiritual. I picked up a book by a woman who wrote about her own adventures into enlightenment. By the cover, it looked like a fantasy novel, which was good, because I still had not told anyone about my vision or how I was beginning a new search into my own spirituality.

The author was herself in the stories, and she became the initiate. She sought truth through her adventures. She told of an initiation where she drank an elixir that put her into a deep trance, all the while wearing a ceremonial mask to cover her eyes. While in trance, she had a vision of an old woman talking to a young girl. She began to realize that the old woman was her and also the young girl. The young girl was asking the older woman to give her all the wisdom that she had within her.

She kept saying, "Grandmother, tell me all you know, for you are so wise!"

The Grandmother told her that in time she would know, but the young girl did not want to wait. She kept insisting that she needed to know now and continued to plead, "Grandmother, please tell me all that you know now, I feel like I am wasting time!"

At that moment, my vision began to unfold.

The Grandmother spoke, "Dear one," she said, "there is no such thing as wasted time, for we live in a dual world—a physical world and a spiritual world. Living our lives in the physical realm gives us our foundation to build and go into our spiritual world."

I jumped out of bed and was about to scream for the whole world to hear, but I realized that my husband would not understand. He was also in bed reading, and whenever I would suggest one of the metaphysical books I was interested in, he would just say, "Why are you reading that junk?" or he would laugh and say, "I am not going to read that crap!"

At this point I didn't care what he thought because it became very clear to me what my vision meant when I was screaming to God that night over a year before.

I hadn't been "wasting time"! I had been living my experiences to create wisdom, so I can make other choices and better choices for my soul's own evolution. How wonderful to know this! What a relief! I wondered what would happen next!

Little did I know then how this moment marked a time of transition into a new life, and a new path, where I would continually fertilize the ground I walked on for my soul's enhancement.

My husband and I were already growing apart at that point, and eventually we divorced, after which I was free to pursue my heart's desire. I was then able to focus less on material things and more on a spiritual journey.

I became more aware that this lifetime was just a blink of an eye and my soul is eternal. It was my responsibility to make sure that every moment I had was to explore more experiences here on Earth, which in turn would expand my soul!

6... It's All Relative

When you dream of a relative, this part of the dream means that it is relative to you. When I dream of my son, what is relative to me is what I love the most, but a son in a dream also means the "sun", our solar plexus within us, loving our power.

My son has always been a joy to me, from the very first day we met. I could swear he smiled at me when he was first placed into my arms. When I told my parents and my in-laws, they told me that it was just gas. What did I know—I was only a kid myself! It wasn't until he was about two weeks old that I decided that it wasn't just gas—he was indeed smiling at me. Of course, I did not tell anyone—it was our secret.

Among all the scary things I have done in my life, nothing compares to the day the nurse handed me my son and told me that I could now take him home. I shook like a leaf, and I could not imagine how I could possibly be responsible for a whole new life, but he made it easy. Often people would say, "Just wait until he gets into the terrible twos or the troublesome threes, or wait until he's a teenager or goes to college." So far, I am still waiting, and he has been nothing but tremendous in my life. I hope I have been the same for him. He definitely came in to be the buffer in my marriage and the light of my life. I am truly grateful for his gift of being my son.

If you had met my son along the way or even today, you would say what a wonderful, nice person he is. He always greets everyone with a great smile. Sometimes I knew that my way of living embarrassed him and that he often wished I was the normal Mom and did normal things that he remembered while he was growing up, but at some level, he understood that I needed to be who I was, which I think allowed him to be whoever he was as well.

Many people have asked me over the years, "How did you get this way? Aren't you afraid people are going to think you are crazy?"

I always reply, "I used to be normal, and then I got bored."

At some deep level my son knew this about me and accepted it.

Now you know where the title came from. I've had many a friend or client wish I would put that on a bumper sticker. Maybe one day, I will!

To show you my son's sense of humor, one morning I was reading a Deepak Chopra book. In the introduction he explained how he never told his children to be the best at what they do, but just to find their gifts and live their dreams. He always told them that he would support them until they did. Even with him never telling them to be their best, they still got straight A's in school and became good at whatever they put their minds to.

As I was reading this, my son was descending the stairs, and I asked him to come and sit with me. He asked, "What's up Mom"?

"Michael," I said. "I want to apologize for not being a better parent. I wish I had known to be more supportive of you finding your gifts."

He looked straight ahead and said, "Mom, can I sue you"?

My jaw dropped. Here I was apologizing for not being a good-enough parent, and he wants to sue me?

"Sue your father–he has all the money!" I jokingly snapped back.

"I would, but you know Dad—he never admits to doing anything wrong. I thought maybe I could get some money out of this, since you admit you did do something wrong."

"You better get out of here, before I throw this book at you!" He laughed as he ran out of the room.

Another time I was ironing upstairs in my bedroom, and he came up the stairs and said, "I just saw a very funny comedian on TV who said, 'You know why parents can always push your buttons? It is because they are the ones who put them there!'

We both laughed, and then I stopped and said, "Wait a minute. Are you saying I put buttons in you?"

"Yes, of course—you and Dad!"

I thought to myself, "Shoot, I really tried hard to not put buttons in him, as my parents did to me, but I guess no matter how you try, it still happens." If only I could have been an aware parent sooner, but we can only be where we are until we decide to change.

He has helped me laugh at myself and the world around me, which I often took too seriously—especially when I was younger. How differently I saw the world then, compared to how I see it now —it is all only an illusion anyway.

So today I choose to learn my lessons with love and laughter — this is what I ask for, and this is what I get. You may be wondering how I came to that conclusion. One day I was in great emotional pain, which was causing me physical pain. I said to myself, "Why do we need to learn from pain? No pain, no gain? Who came up with that one? It permeates our culture. I never liked pain, and who does?"

Then I thought that maybe I just don't need to ask that question. I told myself that just because we accept an old belief as being normal, isn't it about time we rid ourselves of ideas that no longer serve us? Doesn't Spirit want us to be happy, or is it true that we need to suffer here, so we can get into Heaven? Didn't Jesus tell us to "create Heaven on Earth"? Wasn't the Garden of Eden here on Earth? And we keep saying that we need to get back to the garden?

This old belief that we need to learn from pain is so ingrained in us that I couldn't imagine how I could change it in me. I remembered a phrase that people often said about how we dwell on our stories and continuing telling them until we bore others, then we finally bore ourselves, and then we move on. Well, I finally got bored with this idea and then it struck me—just ask for help and guidance. How simple! It worked for me before, why not now? So I asked! And I received.

How do I receive? I pay attention to my dreams and to whatever and/or whoever comes to me on my path/journey, etc. I believe that it all has meaning and importance. As Buddha said, "I'm simply awake"! How simple is that? When we are awake, we observe *everything* that comes our way.

At first I started waking up from dreams laughing! In my dream I would meet a person who I knew was there to teach me something, and then, when they became agitated and controlling, it became funny, like watching a bad movie that got so bad that it was funny!

For example, a year after my divorce, I started dating a spiritual man, and on our first date, we went to a spiritual gathering at his friend's home. By the end of the evening, I was wondering if he was someone who would commit to a relationship or just another guy who would be around for a short while. I quickly received my answer. He went to get our coats, and on his way toward me, as he was holding my jacket, a friend of his asked him, "Hey man, how do you feel about commitment?" He virtually shook before he answered, not intentionally, but his body shook from head to toe. I am not sure that anyone else saw it, but I definitely did. Then he said, as he looked at me, "Ah, OK!" I practically laughed out loud! Look what I drew to myself! In earlier years, I might have mentally beaten myself up about how I only bring men into my life that couldn't commit. Now, at this stage of my life, I saw how funny it was. I knew I chose this, and I can choose something else. More importantly, I knew that he was someone that came on my path to teach me something, so I did not go running for the hills. On the contrary, I enjoyed the ride and learned what I needed to learn with love and laughter!

After gaining this awareness in my life, I looked back on my earlier life and saw how I created things then too. The only difference was that what I created back then fit into the life I desired at that time, when my desires changed, what I created followed suit.

When my son was about 10, I had recurring dreams of being a bird and flying over the Grand Canyon and other various landscapes. Since I pay attention to my dreams, I believed that I needed to learn to fly, especially since I loved being in planes and traveling. Little did I know, at the time, that I was actually feeling trapped in my marriage, and in the life I created, while all along, my spirit wanted to fly.

When I mentioned learning to fly to my then—husband, he thought it was a great idea, and he bought a discovery flight for my anniversary present. The first time I got into a small plane, it was a Cessna 152, which is a two-seater single engine. My pilot became my co-pilot, and that is why it is called a discovery flight. While you are in the pilot's seat, you discover whether or not you really can handle flying a plane.

Merv, my trainer, put me through all the possibilities that I might encounter while flying on my own. It was exhilarating! I loved it and Merv who had been flying for more than 40 years, said that I was a natural. I continued my training, and it was the best thing I could have done for myself. It built my self-confidence in ways I could have never imagined were possible.

I think partially why my husband was supportive was because he and his buddies loved going on golfing trips, and he thought I could fly them anywhere, any time. I didn't necessarily feel used by him—I was just glad to be validated for once. This was an area where I had a valued skill.

One day, one of my husband's friends asked me, "Why are you learning to fly"? He was a local big shot and one of the richest businessmen we knew.

"I simply want to learn," I told him.

"Did your Dad fly a plane"?

"No"! I said.

Then he asked, "Does your husband fly"?

"No."

"Do you have brothers that fly?"

"No," I responded, getting annoyed.

"Well, you're the first woman I have ever met that does not have a father, husband, or brother that flies. Usually, the only reason women learn to fly is because they have a man in their life that has flown."

From then on he seemed to look at me with a lot more respect, and it seemed that I looked at him with a lot less.

It was certainly typical of the era and the area I grew up in. A woman doing something on her own because of her own desires was not normal, which is exactly why learning to fly helped me so much to literally spread my wings and fly. And...it certainly wasn't boring.

When my son was around 12, he asked me, "Mom, why is it that you do 20 things at once and then when one thing is accomplished, 10 more things come in for you to do?"

At first, I felt, "Wow, he does notice that I can accomplish and handle multiple things all at once!"

Then I stopped, and thought, "Yeah, why is it that I need to accomplish and handle multiple things, and when one is accomplished, I jump to the tasks of accomplishing more?"

He made me realize that I needed to prove my worth – that I always had to be a good Mom, a good wife, a good neighbor, a good sister, a good daughter, and good sister-in-law, a good co-worker, etc. Why did women always think they had to be Superwomen?

Talk about becoming awake! Since then, I have let go of requiring approval by anyone in my life. I have learned to approve of myself and know that I AM approved of by the entire Universe! As women, it will be helpful if we remember that we don't have to excel at everything in our lives to be valued.

7... Growth

This leads to blossoming and the flow of beings into new forms. Your will must be clear and controlled and your motives correct.

I was looking for infinitely many simultaneous life experiences, to freely choose triumph or tragedy, at will. I read something like that in a book, but don't remember who, where or when, but I knew that it made sense to me, especially while I was a career counselor.

My time as a high school career counselor was coming to a close. A new Superintendent had been hired, and everyone said that they were excited about him and what he could bring to the School District. When I first met him, I felt that his smile was fake. I did not feel good near this man but thought that I would give him the benefit of the doubt.

In a short time period, my feelings proved true. He was politically motivated and could care less about our students' education. I protested and was immediately asked to write about my job description and send it to him. When I first got hired, my description would have taken one page. After being there nine years, I had successful career programs established, such as a community TV show I created with the students so we could interview local residents about career choices and share it with the public, individual career programs for special kids, and working with teachers to have career programs as part of a student's grade, I had also established shadowing programs, field trips to colleges and tech schools and supplying the school with expert speakers to talk to the students about careers.

It went on for several pages. As I wrote it all I thought was "boy, they were not paying me enough!" But in reality, all along it was obvious to me that it wasn't about payment it was about educating the kids and parents.

When the Superintendent got my job description he was impressed, but decided that I needed to be put into a category. The categories that existed would either eliminate some of my benefits or give me the same benefits that I already had, with more education in a few years. He also informed me that the computers I had asked for to help make my job easier and the students more educated, would not fit into the budget.

Since I was overworked anyway, that did not particularly upset me very much until I found out that the computers went to one of his buddies across the hall. Now, if I knew they would benefit the students, I would have not been so upset. You see, his buddy across the hall was using two of the three computers to run sports gambling pools throughout the school district. When I mentioned something to someone about this, all they said to me was, "You have a problem with this?"

Emotionally I had given up, because continuing to be there was starting to cause physical problems in my body. My job—and this whole place—were literally making me sick!

I remembered when my son was just a baby and I had a job that I hated, but I worked there for the money. I got sick from it as well. I kept dwelling on how much I hated being there and how boring it was. "It was turning my mind into mush," and there was nothing creative or challenging about it. I swore that I would never have a job again just to make money! I also learned that I was focusing my energy on "this job is making me sick!" So I got sick! Pain or pleasure is where you put your attention. What I like or love has taught me to be happier, thus healthier.

I handed in my resignation. From that day forward, I began to focus on what I would love to do and I kept asking myself that question over and over, "What would I love to do?"

I still wanted to work with kids, but I wanted to be free to create something without being stifled by institutional rules. I also wanted to make my own hours and get paid what I knew I was worth. I asked God/Universe to help. Within two weeks, I got a phone call from a CEO of a huge engineering firm who told me that he wanted to give something back to the community. He said that he wanted to start a mentoring program for underprivileged kids who had potential to get out of the ghetto. I was highly recommended to him by the local school district, especially by the guidance counselors.

He asked if I could come to his office and discuss employment. I felt this was what I had asked for, so I met with him the next day. He said that he didn't have the time to put this program together, but he could get support for monies until, hopefully, the government would take up the support. He informed me that I would have a free hand in creating this program, make my own hours, and work with kids and potential mentors in the community, but the pay would be less then I wanted.

I had a decision to make: This was everything that I wanted, but did I have to work for less again? As I was sitting in front of his expensive desk in his large office overlooking the city below, I said to myself, "For what I know I am worth, and for what I am asking for, he could pay me out of his petty cash draw."

What I said was, "I would love having this job, but you need to come up with more money for me or get yourself someone else."

I could see in his face that he was not a happy puppy, but to my surprise he said, "We will see what we can do." And he did!

I really enjoyed my new job, but after six months I was feeling that I wanted to do something new. I truly enjoyed having a free hand in this creation, and the program was very successful, but I felt bored at times.

After the first year of the Mentoring Program, the CEO came to me and said that the monies for the program were getting low, and would I consider a pay cut until he could find more support within the community.

Looking back, this appears to be a co-creative process between me, the CEO and possibly the community. Was I bored because it was time for me to move on? Was their less money available in order to move me on and/or to shift the program? All I know is that I was needing something new and the Universe brought all the pieces together.

Also, by this time, I had decided to stop my exploration of metaphysics, put the books down and apply my knowledge. I needed to have new creative experiences, and explore how easy it might be to manifest to experience life in many forms?

Little did I know at the time just how much I would use our innate ability to create what we want.

8... Creating a New Adventure

According to Druid tradition, the stag stands in front of the Gateway to new beginnings,. When you are contemplating new projects, the stag enables you to feel calmer and draw strength from its Spirit to gain and maintain your independence.

"What would I love to co-create with Spirit?" This was the new way I rephrased the question of what did I want to do. I had moved into a place where I knew I would never create anything by myself.

I realized that I would love being in charge of my own business so my creativity would not be limited by others' limitations! I imagined gathering people together in a comfortable smoke-free atmosphere, listening to live music without having to be in a bar, enjoying good food and good conversations, and looking at beautiful artwork—a place where spiritual people could feel safe to be open and express themselves! How could I put all of this together?

Shortly thereafter I received a phone call from my nephew in California, who mentioned the popularity of coffee houses. I am not much of a coffee drinker—I much prefer water and some teas, but the idea intrigued me. I did more research, and I found that I could create a comfortable place where people could converse and enjoy light meals (salads, soups, *etc.*) and various healthy drinks, hear live music on Friday and Saturday nights, and have a place where local artists could display their work.

The only problem that kept coming up at the time, was that people love their cigarettes with their coffee/tea.

Anytime it was mentioned, I said, "I won't work in a place all day and into the night, having to breathe in other people's smoke. Plus, the artwork would suffer, so they'll just have to smoke outside."

"Well, you'll probably lose business," was often the reply.

But, as it turned out, I had people who smoked and thanked me for having the courage to go smokeless. In all the time I had the Comfy Chair, only one person left in a huff because he could not smoke. Even the musicians, who are notorious smokers, thanked me for going smokeless. They even said that it was the first time they could have their kids come to hear them play.

It was a fun place! I chose the name because I wanted something that put a smile on people's faces and gave them an idea of what the atmosphere may be like. I came up with "The Comfy Chair Coffee House," from an old Monty Python skit. "Oh, no, not the comfy chair!"

The building I found was perfect, a little off the beaten track of Main Street. There was not very much money but I knew that I would manifest whatever I needed. It became fun with that in mind.

Having the name helped me to visualize what it might look like, and I found a building with an old architectural front. I just had to make sure to comply with the city codes.

The bathroom and kitchen needed updating, and a friend did the plumbing for me. The biggest challenge was the stove. I needed a hood that was up to code—4' x 4' and stainless steel. After two months of manifesting comfy chairs, tables, kitchen equipment, electrical fixtures and plumbing work, I had two weeks until opening, but I had only $250 left from the little seed money I had to start.

During this time, people came to me and asked what was going on, and, when I told them, they contributed along the way. Even the mail carrier came in one day and handed me $1,000 as a gift because she wanted to enjoy this new atmosphere that I was creating along her route.

With the pressure of having to get a hood, I called various places that might have what I needed. The only one I could find cost $1,200, and they would deliver it in four days, C.O.D. I ordered it praying that the money would be here. I trusted that all would be good, and I went about other matters at hand.

One day we were painting with the front door open for ventilation, and an older gentleman came to the door and looked up at the old air conditioner in the window above the door.

I smiled and asked how I could be of help to him. He said that he does not usually drive on this street, but today he decided to do so and noticed something happening to this old building so he had to stop by. He questioned me on what I was planning to do with it. I told him, and he said that my air conditioner would be inadequate. I said, "Probably so, but it will have to do for now." He further told me that he had a bigger air conditioner that would do the job, and he would sell it to me for only $100. I knew that this would be a good deal and asked him how and why he would sell it to me at such a low price, and I quickly added, "Does it work?" He informed me that he was a retired electrician, that over the years he had accumulated a variety of items that he fixed and sold, and that he needed to get rid of a lot of things, or his wife threatened to divorce him.

I joked with him that he would not happen to have a hood somewhere in those various items he was trying to get rid of?

"Well," he said, "I think I have a hood, but I don't know if it would meet your needs." At that moment, I thought to myself, how incredible it would be if he happened to have a hood that would meet my needs!

He gave me his address and directions to his house and we arranged for me to stop by the next day. I ended up not only buying the hood, which was perfect and only cost me $50.00, but I also bought the air conditioner, a vintage clock and a variety of other items for a grand total of $250.

After I gave him the money, I remembered that he had mentioned being a retired electrician. I told him that my father had also been an electrician, and I asked if he had known my dad, who had passed away two years earlier.

I told him my dad's name and he said, "Yes, your Dad was an old friend of mine. He was a good man and a good electrician. Sometimes we even worked together on bigger jobs. I was sorry to hear about his death."

I hesitantly said, "Maybe my dad led you to me."

"Yes," he said, "maybe he did."

At that moment I felt in my heart that it was, and I said, "Thanks, Dad!"

When it came to hiring people to work at the Comfy Chair, I just advertised what I wanted to the Universe. Then, when someone came in and asked about working there, I would interview them on the spot, and if it felt right, I would hire them.

One of these hires was Brenda the cook who came to us months earlier. She was great at first, but lately she was getting a little "bitchy" and demanding. I could feel her frustration and she began playing a power game with me. I had given her reign over the kitchen, but then she wanted to also control the rest of the Comfy Chair.

Another game she played was her attraction to my then boyfriend. I knew that he wasn't interested in her, but she kept trying. I wasn't concerned about the boyfriend matter, but she was affecting business with her constant control issues.

One Monday I was planning the rest of the week, including catering for a few local small-business meetings we had that week.

She came out of the kitchen, smiling from ear to ear. At first, I was pleasantly surprised at her change in attitude, but then she threw the bomb! She said that she had found another job and was giving notice. I was a little shocked at first and yet relieved at the same time. I said that I was sorry to lose her (after all she was a great cook), but that I was happy for her new opportunity. I would get busy finding someone to replace her before she left in two weeks, and would she mind helping train the new person?

"You don't understand," she said. "Today is my last day, and I will work to the end of today and not return." When she saw the energy drain out of my face, her smile got bigger.

"Couldn't you give me a little more time?" We had a few catering jobs lined up, and I had no one to cook the breakfasts and lunches.

"That's not my problem," she said. I could feel my stomach tighten and fear rise up, but then, as I saw her smile get larger, I felt myself getting stronger! I thought to myself, "She thinks she has me beat, but I can cook, if I had to, until I could hire someone." I thanked her as calmly as I could for finishing out the day. She was very smug and happy with herself as she floated back to the kitchen.

I said, "Universe, you know what I need!" I went to work, knowing that all would be well.

The day got busier, but after the rush there was the usual down time. I welcomed a young man who walked in through the door. He said, "I'm Louie. I've wanted to come into this place, and I've heard good things about it. I've always wanted to cook in a place like this."

"What do you do now?" I asked. He said that he was in-between jobs, taking courses at the local college.

"Would you like to work here? I need a cook." His mouth dropped open, and he asked when he could start.

"Today."

"OK. Go back into the kitchen and introduce yourself to the cook. It's her last day. Ask her to show you around."

He was glad to do so. I felt kind of sorry for him, tossing him into Brenda's lair, but it truly felt good to be able to show the cook that I, with Spirit's help, could handle any situation she threw my way, and it all happened so quickly! She should have known, since she had witness how I had co-created with the Universe. But we all need to learn our lessons in our own time, including me. And Brenda and I taught each other several things.

A few short minutes later, I heard loud banging noises of pots and pans, cabinet doors slamming, and out he flew.

Louie came over to me and said, "I don't think today is a good day to be in the kitchen."

"I'm sorry. You are probably right. I was hoping she'd be a little more cooperative. Why don't you return in the morning. I'm sure you can find your own way around the kitchen."

"That sounds good. See you bright and early," he said as he flew out the door.

Despite his ordeal the previous day, he showed up on time and began rearranging the kitchen according to his needs and likes. I gave him full charge of introducing new menus, which delighted him.

Louie turned out to be easy to get along with, creative, fun and a great cook!

One year around when spring was just around the corner, I felt that people would be more weight conscious, and instead of eating lunch, they might walk on their lunch breaks and maybe just eat something light. I got the idea that if I could find someone locally who made good frozen yogurts, it might bring such people into the Comfy Chair on their walks.

Again, I focused on what I needed, released it and I got back to the business at hand. I did happen to mention this to Louie, the cook, on his way to preparing for the morning crowd. Within 20 minutes, a man came in on his way to work at a law firm that was just down the street. He mentioned that he had heard great things about our place and wanted to check it out himself. He asked for flavored coffee and a Danish. As we were conversing, I gave him a calendar of events for the month so he could bring his family and friends in for some great entertainment, and food on the weekends.

He thanked me, saying that he would definitely be back soon. On his way out, he stopped and returned to where I was standing. He handed me one of his clients' cards, a young man who was just getting started in the homemade ice cream and yogurt business. He said that his client can provide free samples, which he highly recommended. He hoped that I would call this person to do business.

I thanked him, and he walked out the door, promising to return with friends and family.

Louie emerged from the kitchen with his mouth open, exclaiming his disbelief of what had just happened. "I can't believe it! You only just mentioned to me 20 minutes ago that you wanted to bring in homemade frozen yogurt, and then some guy walks in and tells you where to get it!"

"Yeah, what a hoot!"

"How do you do that?"

"It's simple, I trust."

After a few years, I was once again ready to move on to a new adventure. When I closed the Comfy Chair, some people asked if I was sorry to have experienced it, since I lost money on the venture.

"No," I would answer. "I see it as a successful venture. I was able to live a dream that was but a thought in my head at one time. Money comes and goes, but to live a dream, that's the gain!"

And I think of all the wonderful experiences I learned from having it—all of which contributed to my soul growth!

9... Cathars from a Past Life?

Reincarnation represents the belief that the soul is reborn into a physical body. What is the soul but a form of energy? "

Energy never dies, it just changes form." –Einstein

One day, a very tall man with a very long beard came into the Comfy Chair. Al told me that he was passing through, and he wanted to give a deep-breathing demonstration to my clients. He said that he was living in an ashram somewhere in Oregon for a few years. This is where his teacher introduced him to this deep-breathing technique that helps one go to deeper levels of consciousness. Al offered to demonstrate this to me in a private session. I told him that we could set up an appointment, at my home, when my roommate was out, which gave us the space to get to deeper levels of consciousness. We agreed on the day and time.

Al brought with him his massage table, and we set it up in my living room. I lay down on it, face up. The breathing exercise he instructed me to do was hard for me. Al told me to breathe deeply, all the way down into my belly button. The more deeply I breathed, the more he coached me. After several minutes of this, it felt very uncomfortable, almost painful. I wanted to stop, but Al continued to encourage me. I continued until I finally relaxed and went into a deep trance. It felt like when you are just awakening but are not yet quite awake.

I began to *see* that I was walking at night, through a forest. I felt different; my body was different, and as I looked down, I saw that I was wearing some kind of long robe that seemed to be tied at my waist with a rope that had several knots tied from one of the hanging pieces. I realized that my feet were large and that I wore some sort of sandals. It was clear that I was a man.

I told this to Al, and he asked me to go on. He asked, "Where are you?"

It was like speaking out loud in a dream, "In France."

"What year is this?" he inquired.

"1240 or 1244, I am not quite sure, maybe 1249?"

"What is your journey?"

"I am walking through the woods; I am walking over a small half-moon shaped wooden bridge. I am heading toward a cathedral. There are people inside waiting for me. I come to the entrance, but I can't make myself go in. I feel sad and upset. I have a great deal of love for them. I know they are waiting for me, but I can't go in. I leave and walk further on to my house in the woods, and know I will wait there."

Al asked me to go back to before I was in the woods. I saw myself standing in front of a Pope, who was sitting on his throne with about four men standing around him. They were whispering things to him, and he was staring at me all the while they were talking to him. I felt angry! When the Pope finally spoke to me, he said, "You must renounce all that you have told them!"

"But, Your Eminence, I cannot renounce what I know is true!"

"Renounce all, or they will be burned as heretics!"

"You can prevent their deaths! Just go back and tell them you mistook the text as truth!"

"But, I can't, Your Eminence, I love them with all my heart, I cannot lie to them!"

Once again I was told what to say, and all the while, I was thinking how this man and his counselors do not care about these people.

"Bastards!" I thought, but I also knew that the people's lives were in my hands. I promised to renounce everything for their sake.

Al then asked me to move to another place and time. He wanted me to go back to my house in the woods, where I was waiting.

I saw men barge into my small, humble lodge and take me to a foreboding place where they imprisoned me, but not before I was beaten and tortured. They decided not to kill me until after they were able to hunt down the rest of my people. This way, I would not be considered a martyr. As time went on, I prayed and meditated every day in my cell, and they were happy to inform me of all my people they hunted down and burned at the stake. Story after story made me feel numb inside, and I kept praying for my dear friends and family.

One day, one of my captors asked, "Piffre, what have you done wrong? I have been watching you, and I believe you are a good man, a man of God. What could you have done to make the Pope and his advisors so angry with you?"

"My friend, we simply have different points of view."

After that, this man asked me more questions that I answered, and I found a little more bread to eat each time. His voice became softer, and we would talk about God's love and forgiveness. Our talks seemed to comfort him.

This conversation got back to the Pope and his advisors, who then condemned me to death because they felt it was now safe to do so.

I was brought to a stone slab, held down by two of my captors and my friend, who was standing over me with a sword in hand. Even though he wore a hood to cover his face, I still recognized him. His hand was shaking as he held the sword. He hesitated.

I said, "My friend, it is all right, do your job and do it well."

He drove the sword into my heart. I could feel the cold blade enter, then a shock of pain, then there was warmth, and then I was out. I floated out of my body, looked down and saw my body there, lying on the slab of stone with all three men around me, watching as I died.

I kept floating upward. I heard angelic voices, and I saw a host of angels reaching and guiding me, pulling me through the ceiling and up above the clouds. I was happy and joyous.

Al told me to slowly feel myself back in my body, then to feel the table underneath me, then to open my eyes.

He wrote everything down that I had said. I asked him, "Are you aware of any people in the mid 1200's that were put to death?"

"No, sorry, I'm not," he replied.

I couldn't let this go, so I began my research in the local library. All I could find was a small paragraph that said, in the mid 1200's a group of people called the Abigensians were considered heretics by the Roman Catholic Church. That is all I could find at that time and from my catholic school teachings, I knew that once the Church considered you a heretic, there was no questioning as to why. Every once in awhile, I researched some more, but I did eventually find the answers by a different series of events that led me to France.

A sect of Christians called Cathars concentrated near Albi, France, which led them to be known as Albigensians. They called themselves Katharos, which means "Pure Ones." Catharism, which emanated from Asia Minor in the 10th century, was particularly and warmly received among the people, and, as a result, when the Church became ostentatious about its wealth and its priests were leading dissolute lives, the Cathars–poorest of the poor, and leading ascetic lives–soon became a very real threat to the Church and to the Kingdom.

The Cathars did not ask the nobles/elites for money, as they did not encourage tithing to their Church, a principle that had never been accepted in the area. Above all, after conquering the elite, the Cathars won the heart of the people, who appreciated lack of riches among ecclesiastics, admired their exemplary life, and understood their teachings, which were given in common language. Women were given respected and equal roles in the Cathar Church. The Pope, therefore, with the support of the King of France inaugurated a Crusade which was part of the Inquisition, against the so-called heretics, an agony that was to last for nearly half a century.

In the Languedoc region, their last stand was at Montsegur. A community of Cathar women had already become established on the mountain by the end of the 12th Century. At the beginning of the 13th Century, the Cathars asked Raymond de Pereille, the local nobleman and landowner at the time, to construct a defensible building out of the existing ruins of Montsegur. From 1232 on, the castle became the headquarters of the Cathar Church and the refuge of noblemen who found themselves dispossessed by the crusades.

On March 1, 1244, the besieged occupants made an abortive attempt to escape, and on the following day they surrendered. The Cathars were given 15 days respite, at the end of which they had to choose to either renounce their beliefs, or be burned at the stake. On March 16, 1244, hundreds of Cathars were burnt alive, and the name Montsegur became a legend.

When I finally got to France and climbed Montsegur, I was surprised to feel joy instead of sorrow. I believe that was so because there was much joy in these people's lives. The love that I felt in my vision was what I felt while there. At the top, I looked across and saw a cave opening. I felt that I wanted to go there.

When we got back to the little village of Montsegur, I asked the gentleman behind the gift shop counter, where I bought a book, "Was there ever a Cathedral around here?"

"No," he said.

"Well, can you tell me about the cave that I saw at the top of Montsegur?"

"Well," he said. "Actually that cave was called Cathedral Cave because when you go inside, it reminds one of a Cathedral."

"How can I get there?"

"Just go down this road and there is a path that will take you into the woods. You cross over a small bridge and continue up the hill through the woods until you get to the entrance of the cave. Unfortunately, you cannot enter the cave. The French government closed it to the public because people were taking pieces of the cave drawings with them."

I did go down the road and through the woods and came to a half moon shaped bridge—the one that I saw in my vision, only this one was not made of wood any longer. It had the same shape but was cement. I just knew that I had been here before.

When I guide clients to a past-life experiences, I tell them that it is not about holding onto the past. There is a reason why our soul's memory is showing us a particular time and place from this past life. I believe it is to show us that we are more than who we think we are in the present, or to take away a gift that we developed in the past that we could be using now. It could also be to release a fear, or to understand why we are recognizing or feeling close to someone we have met or are related to in this life's experience.

How did this memory change me? In many ways, the gift I gained was to know that I could speak in front of a large group of people without fear. In this life, to speak in front of even a small group of people, frightened me. I also realized that several people I felt close to in this life, were ones I knew from that life. How, you ask? The energy I felt from the captor who became my friend while I was imprisoned was the same energy that I feel talking to a dear friend I now know, for example.

Another gain was the wonderful people I had the pleasure to meet while researching and exploring along the way and while I was in France. The knowledge I gained from getting to know Catharism was astounding, especially since I had no idea that it and the people who created it, even existed! As I said, once you were pronounced a heretic by the church, you were considered dead to the world, and anyone who wrote or talked about you also became dead. So where are the scrolls and writings about these people and their religion? In time, I was told, all will be revealed!

10... Crow Woman

 *In a dream a Crow means to shape shift that old reality and become your future self. Strive to live the ordinary life in a non-ordinary way.*

It was time for something new to come into my life, but what? Since I did not have very much money, after I closed the Comfy Chair, I asked for guidance to give me advice on what to do. I had arrived at a place where my visions and dreams seemed to be coming true faster—I'd have a dream, and the next day it would come true.

I have found that as I travel on this beautiful planet of ours, for me, sometimes the energies of particular places combined with my energies have created faster manifestations.

On one adventure, I had to drive almost 2,000 miles before I found a place that felt right. The altitude there was 8,600' above sea level with spectacular views from my hotel suite. What a great place it was and it felt like home for the first time in my life! I couldn't wait to get out into nature, so I decided to go for a walk on one of the trails that led through the tall trees. I never felt afraid; I followed my instincts and guidance. The more I walked, the more aware of my surroundings, I became. At first, I noticed the different colors of leaves on the trees, the shapes of the trees here and the brilliant blue sky peering through the top branches. As I walked, I noticed all the foliage on the ground, which made me feel refreshed, clean and uplifted, as if I just stepped out of a shower. I felt the warm breeze against my face, the comforting sun embracing me. I embraced it all and felt like the earth and sky were putting strong arms around me and pulling me close to its embodiment. I was receiving a wonderful gift!

As I continued on, I also touched the various textures of the barks and leaves. I thought about a book I had read that talked about American Indians and their communication with Nature. I wondered if I could do this, so I became silent and still. I listened to the leaves rustling in the trees, the birds singing near-by, and the different sounds in the distance. I closed my eyes and heard a soft voice. I then heard it again, and over to my left was an image. It seemed like there was light around it. As I got closer, the image turned into a figure of an old Indian woman, with long white hair with strands of black running through here and there. She wore a beaded headband mostly, white with red and turquoise beads in a pattern. She had beautiful soft brown eyes and a gentle smile. She wore a buckskin dress with beaded designs at her shoulders. I was startled to see her there, but only for a second or two, for there was no fear, and her presence almost felt comforting, as if I was seeing an old friend standing there, waiting for me to recognize her.

"Oh, hi!" I said, "I was startled at first to see you there, but I was not expecting to see anyone else on my walk. You seem familiar to me, do I know you?"

Even as I was saying this, I knew we had never met before, but her familiar smile and soft eyes were captivating. The old woman spoke, but her lips did not seem to move. It was as if her voice was inside my head. She said that her name was Crow Woman, and yes, we did know each other. She was with me in another life and had decided not to incarnate in this lifetime, so she could be my Spirit Guide.

"So, you are actually telling me that what I am seeing is spirit and that you do not exist on this plane?"

"Yes," she said.

I'm open to a lot of things, but I blurted out, "This is absurd! I must be going crazy!"

Then I realized that the branches and leaves were moving by the breeze, but she was not being affected—her clothes and hair were still. She seemed so real!

Quietly I said, "I believe in Guardian Angels, but how did you become my Spirit Guide?"

"When we come to Earth, we are given much help from the Great Spirit, because it is difficult here. The Earth and this part of the Universe are still young and have much to learn in order to evolve. We choose to be here to help with its evolution. We come from different parts of the Universe, and even from other universes, to bring forth the wisdom of the ages to help with the evolutionary process. This is happening elsewhere in Creation, because Creation never stops creating. We think that we are the only ones, but as I said, we are young and have much to learn."

"Well, how do I know you?" I said, "Are you saying that I was an American Indian in another lifetime?"

"Yes," she said, "We were from the same tribe, from different parents, but were born into the tribe almost around the same time."

"Oh, we were friends," I said.

"Yes, but no," she said. "You thought we were friends but I was always jealous of your accomplishments. You were everyone's favorite. You always did everything right. You learned fast and gave joy and love to everyone, even to me. As we grew, I became more and more jealous of you, but you did not seem to notice. We all had our responsibilities, because we knew that helping each other made the tribe stronger. The stronger the tribe, the easier it was to survive whatever Mother Earth put into our path. We got to know each other's strengths and weaknesses. We learned to honor our strengths in ourselves and others, and to learn from our weaknesses.

"We had similar gifts, and we could communicate with the spirit world. We both were learning from the shaman of the tribe. He taught us how to use our talents to see into each level of consciousness to know our visions and dreams and how they would help the tribe at times. He taught us how to recognize plants and herbs that could heal and take away pain. He taught us to communicate with nature spirits and animal spirits, and he gave us insights.

"Here again, you seemed to be better than me. There was someone else you had and I did not—a young brave named Moon Hawk. He was beautiful. He loved you and you him. Everyone took this for granted. No matter what I did, you always seem to get what I desired. I hated living in your shadow. When you shined your light, you gave others permission to shine theirs. I resisted your light and became the shadow. I wanted you to just go away, somehow, then, I believed my light would shine and I would be loved by all, especially, Moon Hawk.

"While we learned about different herbs and plants that could cure, I also learned that there were plants that could harm. I experimented with them. You would ask me why was I experimenting and cautioned me, but I told you that I wanted to come up with even better cures. You seemed to think that that was a great idea; you trusted me. One day as we were gathering plants and herbs, you cut your arm. I said that I had one of my cures with me and would you allow me to apply it to your cut. You immediately said yes, and you seemed anxious for me to prove myself. As I applied my treatment, you touched my hand and said that we both were going to help the tribe by becoming great healers, and that our tribe was lucky to have two.

"It did not take long before you were gone. I wondered why I did not feel as good as I thought I would when you left, but I rationalized that everything would be better as soon as the grieving was over. I tried comforting Moon Hawk, but he wanted none of it. Again, I rationalized and felt that after some time, he would see and feel my love and come to me.

"Then one of the elders had a vision that Great Spirit had turned you into an eagle so you could watch over the tribe and help protect it. Soon after this vision was revealed, an eagle appeared daily flying over our tribe.

"Moon Hawk said, 'I too will be an Eagle!' He fell sick and died within a week. Soon after his death another eagle appeared flying over the tribe. You would often see both eagles flying, always together never apart.

"Soon after, my talents and gifts that the Great Spirit gave me were taken away. I could not communicate with nature spirits or animal spirits. I could not remember what herbs or plants did good or harm. I flew into a rage, and I was soon exiled from our people. I walked alone for the rest of my days and learned to scavenge like the crows."

I asked, "So, you are trying to make things right?"

She answered, "I am here to help, protect and guide you on your path. I am also here to help you remember what you learned from that lifetime, to remember the Shamanic ways, the part of you that you forgot. What else do you wish to know?"

"I wish to know what I was called," I answered.

"Your name was, Winter Wild Wind Song. You were born in the middle of winter, when a strong wind was blowing, and it sounded like a song through the trees. You also used the wind while you healed to help cleanse and purify."

"Why have you decided to not incarnate and be my Spirit Guide?"

"Because I needed to rectify the wrong I have done to you and to ask for your forgiveness."

As she spoke to me, I felt in my heart that I have no animosity towards this spirit, and I said so, and if this was what was needed to be here on this beautiful planet, I will be honored to forgive and to be taught by her. She was grateful.

Crow Woman guided me for the next five years. I meditated every morning and when my mind was clear, Crow Woman would appear in my vision and tell me how to work with crystals, sounds, essential oils and animal spirits. Then one day, she told me that eventually she would move on, because she could only teach me to the level of what she knew. I would then be introduced to two more spirit guides who would get me to an even higher level of consciousness. When she did move on, she said that my forgiveness had helped her to forgive herself so she too could move on to a higher consciousness.

After working with Crow Woman and doing what she taught me for my own healing process, I was sought out by friends who asked me to do healings on them. What I was doing seemed helpful, especially, after friends and then their friends kept responding well to my insights and new-found gifts.

I began wondering about what I was going to do next. Then I received a brochure in the mail for a two-week intensive with knowledgeable shamans in a different part of the world. I had a desire to go, but I wondered how I would get there. Then the money came in. I had to write and tell them about myself to be accepted into the program.

On this journey I traveled 3,000 miles. I was surprised to learn that the other 49 students were from other parts of the world and varied in age from 20 to over 80 and almost an even number of men and women. How wonderful that the woman sitting next to me, in our first meeting, was the same age as my mother. What a hoot, to imagine my mother studying shamanism and sitting next to me with a drum in hand!

After getting my assigned cabin, I was tired from the trip, and just wanted to get to bed and try to adjust to the time difference. The rest of the group decided to go down to the hot mineral springs before bed. I finally drifted off to sleep but awoke around 4:00 am. I looked up to the skylight above my bed. As I lay there, staring up at the clear dark cloudless sky, a white whale slowly drifted by, disguised as a cloud. As I watched, I got a message to get up and go down to the hot springs. I thought about this, argued with myself about it for a little while, and then finally gave into the urge. I got dressed in the dark, tried not to make noise because my roommate was sound asleep in the next bed, grabbed a towel, and got my flashlight to find my way down to the hot mineral springs.

The moon was bright, so I could venture down there without too much trouble. When I got there, I was alone. The water felt terrific! The hot springs were located on a cliff above the ocean below. It felt so good, and was just what I needed to do for myself after such a long trip. As the sun started to slowly emerge behind me, I noticed what I thought were fins moving in the ocean below. Then they proved that they were dolphins when a couple of them began jumping out of the ocean. As I looked harder, I saw more dolphins and they were swimming and jumping around as if they were in a huge circle. I was so grateful and thanked god/goddess and my spirit guides for guiding me here to enjoy this wondrous sight. Then I couldn't believe my eyes as I noticed a larger object in the center of the dolphin circle. I realized that it was a whale! I jumped out of the hot springs, joyously crying and being grateful to all for allowing me to be here. I watched for a little while longer, then the whale seemed to disappear and then the dolphins were gone too.

Someone told me later that sometimes dolphins will encircle a whale while she is giving birth. I could not see what was happening because of the distance but I still felt very privileged to have had that experience.

I gathered my things then went back to my cabin. I thought, "If this is just the first day, I cannot imagine what the rest of this trip will be like!"

We went to breakfast, and then gathered for our first session. The woman that sat next to me the night before was absent, her roommate told the class and the teacher that she was not well and when she felt better, she would come to class. It seemed the long trip was a little too much for her.

After the drumming, the male shaman told us that the female shaman would instruct the first session, and he would see us later.

She introduced herself and explained what all was involved with shamanic journeying. Finally, she told us to partner up and after a few minutes of people shuffling around, I found myself partnerless since one person was absent.

As expected, the Shaman woman called out, "Who here doesn't have a partner?" I reluctantly raised my hand.

"Ok, then I'll be your partner."

That struck fear inside of me. Oh, no, great! My first journey and I have to have the teacher as my partner! She knows what to do but I am just learning! Our goal was to do a shamanic journey for our partners and get information for them that would be what they need to know for preparation of the next two weeks.

I got myself as calm as I could and prayed for help. Then the drumming started and we laid down next to each other and went into a trance state to be guided by our Spirit Guides, who would assist us with our journeys. Crow Woman came to my aid and told me to tell the teacher that she was not completely here and to let go of her thoughts that took her away to the people that were staying in her house. I asked Crow Woman, "Can't you give me a nicer message to give to her? After all, she was my first human teacher." She was adamant and said to promise to tell her what I was told and then she would give me another message for her. I promised and then she told me to tell her that the house she was looking for will be found in the area she wants. I thanked Crow Woman for her help and came back from the journey.

The drumming stopped and we were told to share what we received with our partners. She looked at me and asked what information I had for her. I hesitantly told her about her not being completely here and to stop thinking about her house situation.

Then I told her that she would find the house she wants in the area she wants.

She just stared at me, then said, "Your Spirit Guide is absolutely right! I have people staying at my house and my mind has been concerned about them being there."

Then she asked me and said with surprise in her voice, "I will get the house I want in the area I want?"

"Yes," I said.

She was very pleased to hear this but also added, "It won't be too expensive?"

"I would guess not," I replied.

She then told me my message. What she gave me was just as startling.

"I saw an eye of a single whale and this is very unusual since whales travel in pods. This whale was very still and not moving, as if watching, listening and waiting. I asked if the whale had a message for you and the whale told me that you need to be still and listen for the entire two weeks. Be the observer and pay close attention, then you will learn all that you need. After this, your heart will open with a song and the final message was *Be free.*"

I then told the shaman about the morning experience at the hot springs and how I saw the dolphins circling the single whale. She seemed pleased, but not shocked. I guess she sees amazing "coincidences" like this all the time. For me, however, this was just the first day and first session and I was amazed. The shaman did let me know a month later that she did find the house in the area she wanted and it was perfect.

Over the next two weeks, so much happened to confirm what I already learned from Crow Woman and more. Nature spirits spoke to me, and animal spirits came in journeys and dreams. I learned more about my animal totems and the Swan, my heart totem, took me on many journeys. Coyote would help me to laugh at myself and Eagle and White Dove and Raven helped me to fly. Jaguar did not show itself until I studied a few years later with a Peruvian Shaman. The Hummingbird came to me in Jamaica with the African Woman Shaman. When I studied with the Celtic Shaman, I learned more about the Swan and Sea Dragon.

There was one incident that I remember that is still astonishing to me. One morning before breakfast, I decided to go sit and meditate at the waterfalls that flowed into the ocean. I wanted to eat breakfast first and journey to the waterfalls before going to class. Once I got to breakfast, I sat alone at a long table. I started to eat, and then a few of my classmates arrived and asked to sit with me. I said I would be happy for their company, but I was not staying long, for once I finished my meal, I was off to the waterfalls to meditate before class. My plan was thwarted as we all got into a very profound discussion about what we were learning, but periodically my mind would go to the waterfalls and then had to be brought back to the conversation. More of our classmates joined the discussion, and it got more intense. I felt that I could not leave, but I still felt that I could get to the waterfalls before class.

A few times I tried to excuse myself, but I always got pulled back in. I finally surrendered to being with my classmates—a bit disappointed—but I told myself that the next morning I would go first to the waterfalls to meditate and then eat breakfast.

When it was time for class, we picked up our drums and began heading out. Just then, one of my classmates named Virginia came in, and she was a bit rushed. She grabbed her drum and then came over to me.

As she leaned in toward me she said, "I saw you meditating at the waterfalls this morning! I wanted to get your attention, but you were deep in meditation, so I thought I would sit near you and we could walk to class together, when you were done."

I could not believe my ears! "That's impossible, since I've been here the whole time."

"Really? How could that be? I saw you sitting there, but when I was done meditating, I looked for you, but your were already gone."

"That is so strange," I exclaimed, "because it was my intention to go to the waterfalls and meditate this morning but I got caught up with a discussion at breakfast, and I never got there. It must have been someone else that looked like me."

She shot an angry look my way and said, "No, it had to have been you, because no one here has the same hair and jacket like the one you wear."

My hair at that time was down to my butt, plus the jacket I wore was handmade by Native Americans and probably was one of a kind.

I just stood there, knowing that what she was saying was true, but completely dumbfounded by the possibility of it. It was at that time that I opened up to the possibilities of bi-locating.

I wanted to stay in this magical place, but I knew that I had to return home with what wisdom I had learned and share it with all who wanted to know.

However, when I returned home, I wasn't sure how to present what I learned, so I meditated and asked for guidance. The word "Trust" came up. I was then guided to open a healing center to provide services to locals. I argued and said, "How am I going to open a healing center and teach Shamanism in a place which is occupied by people who aren't very open to change and who possess all the fears I was raised with?" Again, the word "trust" came into my vision, and I heard, "When you do this here, in your own birthplace, you can do this anywhere!"

"OK," I said, "I will trust that it is possible, just show me how and where?"

One day, I was talking to my mother about finding a place to do my work. She has never approved of what I was "getting into," because she feared for my soul because of her religious beliefs, but she knew in her heart that I would never do any harm, and I always showed her that I love helping people and have their best interests at heart. She was confused about my choices, but she saw how miracles happened for me and how I trusted my gifts and beliefs. She pointed out that she just happened to see in the local newspaper a place for rent that sounded great. It was on top of a hill overlooking the city below, had one hundred acres mostly trees with an old refurbished stone farm house and barn. When she pointed it out to me, I couldn't believe she of all people, would lead me to what I could not imagine for myself. She strongly suggested that I call and make an appointment to see it, which I did.

I met with the son-in-law of the owner. He told me that the property was purchased as an investment for his children (the only grandchildren) by Doc, his father-in-law. They got it at an auction and refurbished it. They wanted to rent it until his sons were able to take care of it, when they got older. It was perfect! I told him who I was and what I wanted to do there. He would discuss it with his father-in-law and get back to me. The price was more then I believed I could afford, so I meditated and asked for guidance, "Was this the place?"

"Yes," was the answer, and again the word "trust" came to mind.

I had two weeks to come up with the deposit and the first month's rent. I only had a couple of hundred dollars to my name but knew if I dug in my heels and believed that it would happen, it would!

I met Doc, the father-in-law, who was a retired surgeon from the biggest hospital in the area. He seemed to like me and when I told him what I was planning to do on the property, it did not seem to faze him. I signed a two year lease and gave him the little money I had for the deposit and promised the rest soon.

Two weeks of packing went fast, I still did not have the money and it was only two days before the first of the month. I stopped my packing and prayed, I said, "I know you told me to trust, but could you just give me a sign that the money will come and make this wait a bit easier for me?" I went back to packing and felt, I need to trust!

Two hours later I got a phone call from a former client, who lives an hour's drive away. He called to let me know that if I needed his help for the move, he would be glad to participate.

"I am so touched by your gesture, but I have all the help I need for the move especially since you live an hour's drive away, but it is so kind of you to offer your services."

"No," he said, "You don't understand. I called to ask if you needed any financial help with the move. Since you helped me get better employment, I want to share my abundance with you. Then you can help others in the future."

My first impulse was to say, "No", because it wasn't easy for me to accept money without doing a service of some counseling or healing for the exchange. Then I remembered that I asked for a sign, and I knew that the Universe was showing me how, if I would only be open to receive.

I told him, "Yes, that would be wonderful and very generous of you to do so."

Then he asked the tougher question, "How much do you need?"

This I could not say so I just said, "As much as you feel you would like to donate."

He drove the hour to my house and wrote out a check for almost the whole amount. I knew the rest would follow.

With great enthusiasm, I told two of my friends that believed in me, what had just happened, they asked, "How much more do you need?"

I told them and when they heard the amount, they pulled together what they had which gave me the rest with a dollar extra! I moved in, in two days, with their help. I guess what they say is true, "build it and they will come." So it happened!

Growing up, I would watch my Dad, dream a dream and say "When my ship comes in, I will accomplish this or that" or "When I win the lottery or win at the horse races" and then I would watch him get discouraged waiting, working very hard and hoping and then nothing. Before he died, I had the opportunity to sit alone with him and tell him what a wonderful Dad he was and that I was very grateful to have had him as my Dad! He looked up, while he was lying in the hospital and said, "I wish I could have done more."

This memory has given me the courage, not to wait until I get the monies to accomplish my dreams and with help and guidance that I believe is All-Knowing and All-Mighty and All-Loving, I can manifest whatever is for "My Highest Good" and for the good of others.

The purpose of this chapter, I have come to realize, is to paint pictures with my words to give as much insight to you with the stories I have lived, so you too can learn to trust and accomplish whatever your heart desires no matter how difficult it may look and with little monies. With trust in Spirit and *knowing* from within, that all is possible!

11...　House Snake

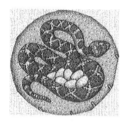

All things are equal in creation, with the proper state of mind, those things considered as poison whether thought, desire or action, can be transmuted. Hermes, the father of alchemy, used the intertwining of two snakes around a sword to represent healing.

My first night in my new house was exciting—so quiet and peaceful. Then I began to hear scratching in the wall behind my bed. It continued, then continued increasing and I realized that I had company. A family of mice already inhabiting this house was letting me know of their presence. I finally fell asleep, but before sleep came, I told myself that I could cohabitate with them and that it would be all right. I believe that all life is sacred and that we are all here to coexist.

The next morning, however, I went to get cereal out of a kitchen cabinet, and I realized that the mice had gotten there first and left me little presents. I threw out the remaining cereal, and I decided to have a talk with the mice. I meditated, got myself centered, and asked to speak to the spirit of the mice. They came in loud and clear.

"Since we are both living here now could you please not eat my food and be so kind as to get your own? And would you please not scurry in the walls of my bedroom at night? I would appreciate the silence."

The mouse spirit informed me that since they were in the house before me, that I should accept their presence and just know that they will continue to do what they have been doing before I got there and maybe I was the one who should leave? I could not believe that they would be so arrogant! One evening, as I was watching TV in the living room, I saw one scurrying along the cable lines that were connected to the TV. It saw me, and then it emerged from behind the TV, came toward me, stood on hind legs about four feet away and looked right at me, as if to say, "I am not afraid of you."

I said, "You are a blatant little thing, aren't you!"

I then prayed and asked the Universe to intervene on my behalf: "Please, talk to the mice, because I do not want to leave this place, and I will not try to kill these mice in any way. It is in your power."

Within a week, I noticed that my new cereal boxes were untouched, and there were no little presents left for me by the mice, nor any noises at night in the walls, and no scurrying on the wires behind the TV.

I said, "Thank you, Universe, for taking care of this matter so quickly!"

Just then I heard a knock at the front door and when I opened it, their stood a big burly man in jeans and a flannel shirt. He was here to clean out the furnace before winter. I showed him the door to the basement and switched on the light for him to descend the stairs.

Within a few short minutes, he called up to me, "Miss, could you come down here for a minute?"

"Are you OK."

"Yes," he replied but can you come down to see something that I found next to the furnace?"

I descended the stairs and there he was, next to the furnace, holding up a long thin object. He seemed very nervous, and he looked around himself as he asked, "Did you know that you have a snake in your basement?" He was holding the recently molted snake skin.

"No, I did not know that." I smiled and said, "Now, I know what happened to the mice!"

He asked again, as he looked around, "So, this is OK with you?"

"Yes," I said, and I went back upstairs. He did not seem calmed by this, and he probably was hoping that I would have helped keep an eye out for him while he was cleaning out the furnace.

A few weeks later, as I was downstairs doing wash, I noticed on the wall next to the dryer, a baby snake crawling up the wall. How wonderful, the mother snake had babies, now I knew that I would never be bothered by mice, as long as I was living here.

I lived in the old farm house for almost four years, and a few days before I left, a mouse came scurrying across the living room floor. He got on his hind legs and seemed to blatantly exclaim, "We're back!" I guess the snake knew to leave when I left.

How can we communicate with Nature and be more interactive? Everything has a spirit, and we are all connected and created with Spirit, so why can't we communicate with everything? A wise man once told me, "Respond to life. Don't react." So, when life came at me, I would not react; I would stop, go within, and ask, "What would be the best response in this situation?"

Even the Bible says, "Ask and you shall receive." It doesn't say only sometimes, or occasionally, or only on a certain day at a certain time! It all began that night in my living room when I cried out to

God and then received a vision. That was when I began to believe in a "Higher Power" again and when I decided to test my ability to trust. I found out that it works! The more I read from other people's experiences, and the more I learned from different philosophies, and Shamans, human or spirit, I would apply what I read or learned to my life to see if it was truth for me.

I took the scientific approach and tested it out by asking Spirit how to respond to everything, every day. This was not easy, because I had always had an inquisitive mind, but I was told as a child, "It is not nice to ask," or I was told by Nuns that "if you ask questions, you're doubting, and when you doubt, you sin. You need to just listen to what you are told and have faith." I don't believe that we should blindly follow anyone or anything that is written – we all need to question anything that does not feel right to us, because, as the song says, "It Ain't Necessarily So!" It's ironic that it isn't always good to listen and follow whatever people tell you, but I have learned to trust in spirit. However, I say this with a word of caution. It is vital to distinguish between Spirit and your Ego or the voices in your head. It takes practice.

Here is the key: When something feels right to us at our deepest level, it is probably right. I understand that not everyone feels that they can communicate with Nature, or even the spiritual aspect within them. I did not feel that I could, because I was closed to it, but when I was feeling alone and unloved, I wasn't feeling much of anything! Then, when I wanted to feel again, not just survive and be "comfortably numb," but really live, I knew that I had to start feeling again without fear or doubt and be more open. Also, if I was going to trust in a "Higher Power," I wanted to believe it with every fiber of my being.

When I said that I took the scientific approach and tested it out, believe me, I tested it out! I put myself in many situations without money and without knowing anyone, and without having anyone's support, just to see if I was still loved and supported by the Universe. Guess what? I am.

"How do I trust so much?" My answer is, "simply by trusting."

"Even when things are at their worst?"

"Yes, I trust from within even more!"

What does trusting from within mean?

It is worth repeating. To me, it means that there is a knowing. By practicing a great deal (that is why it is called a "spiritual practice"), then asking, and then allowing yourself to feel what is true for you, you begin to know. The practice then gives you the opportunity to learn how to trust from within, and not what is outside of you. Then you begin to know without having to ask. I tell clients, "When you just know, you don't have to ask!"

12... Chief of Anger

This Rune calls for a deep probing of the meaning of profit and gain in your life. Look with care to know whether it is wealth and possessions you require for your well-being, or rather self-rule and the growth of a will.

At the healing center, I held celebrations for summer and winter solstice, the fall and spring equinoxes, full moon, etc. For the first summer solstice celebration, I put out fliers all over town and then told the Universe to ensure that whoever showed up had an open mind and open heart. Over 200 people came, some with their children, so the ages ranged from toddlers to elders in their eighties.

There was also almost an even number of men and women, which surprised a lot of the women, because they often asked me, "Where are all the spiritual men?" I told them that when they started believing that there are spiritually awake men out there, then maybe they would start to see some, and they did! People brought lots of food and beverages plus musical instruments. From noon on the Solstice until 3:00 a.m., people came, enjoyed, played, danced, sang and even swam in the pond.

A very tall black man showed up, dressed in cutoff jeans, with neither shirt nor shoes, and the callouses on his feet looked almost two inches deep! I asked him who he was and how he came to be here on this day. He told me that he was born in Texas and that he had a job with a family there. But one day, he heard a voice from God that told him that he needed to let go of everything and walk for peace. He then left everything behind, took his shoes off, and walked all over the U.S., Mexico and Canada in the name of peace. He was walking about 20 miles from the center when he heard a man talking about this Summer Solstice celebration and decided he needed to be here. I told him that I was honored to have him here to help celebrate with us, and that he was very welcomed to share in all the festivities.

"How wonderful for others you have met along the way to have you walking for peace and sharing that with them!"

He looked sad and said, "Not everyone feels that way."

"That was their loss." As the day went on, I saw him enjoying the gathering in various ways, and then, that evening, he was gone.

The next morning, as I was cleaning up outside, a car came down the driveway. As I approached the car, I noticed that there were four men and woman inside, and as I got closer, I realized that the men were Native Americans. The one on the passenger side rolled down his window and asked, "Is this the place where the Summer Solstice is being held?"

I was surprised by the question, and I felt a little disappointed that they missed it by one day.

"Yes, I'm sorry but it was yesterday."

I saw his face become confused and angry. He turned and told the rest of his group, and then all of them were arguing among themselves about who got the date wrong. I then thought to myself, now look at this, the Universe is telling me that they got it wrong, I wondered if it was because they were not coming from open minds and open hearts. I silently thanked the Universe for listening to my request so the celebration could be fun, joyful and without conflict!

With an offer of lemonade on the back porch, I asked how far they had traveled, and who was in their company. The man next to the window answered, telling me that they had driven all the way here from a different state and that their chief was in the back seat with his wife, and yes, they would be glad to have some lemonade. I then unfolded some chairs, but only the chief and his wife sat, while the other men stood next to their chief like sentinels with their arms crossed over their chests. As I sat across from the chief, their body language was saying that they were closing off their hearts to me, and I wondered what they came here to do! I then found out, when the chief spoke with authority.

"Who are you to teach shamanic techniques, and who were your teachers?"

I looked him right in the eye, and said, "No man," (I then looked at his wife) "or woman, is going to tell me what I can and cannot do, when Spirit has guided me and taught me through visions and dreams what it is that I am here to do. You know very well that Spirit is the best and only true teacher!"

His men and wife were astounded that I would talk to him with authority and express myself in that manner. He also was taken aback by my authoritative tone. I kept my eyes on his and thought that neither he nor anyone else was going to intimidate me, for he is only human, like the rest of us on Earth, here to learn and teach as we are guided to do so.

Then he spoke with a calmer voice, "When I was younger and on my vision quest, I was told by Spirit that I am the one to bring the four directions together."

I felt compassion for him, and I said, "You have too much anger in your heart. It will not be possible to bring your vision to fruition until you rid yourself of that anger."

He put his head down, knowing full well that what I was saying was true! That is when his sentinels lowered their arms and sat down on the ground around us.

His wife finally spoke up. You could see that she was embarrassed by it all and wanted to change the subject. She said, "I understand that you have a room filled with crystals. Can I see it?"

At that moment another car came down the driveway, and it was a man from the previous day who had lost an earring and wondered if I had found it. I introduced him to everyone and said to the chief's wife, "Come into my house and I will show you the room filled with crystals."

We left the men to discuss their issues. When I went into my healing room with all the crystals, she stopped at the doorway and said, "My goodness, the energy in this room is tremendous!"

"Come in." I said to her.

She hesitated, then walked into the room and looked at me with sad eyes, saying, "My husband is a good man, but you are right—he does have anger in his heart."

"How are you helping him?"

She did not answer, and I knew why—she felt that since he was the chief, she needed to keep her mouth shut and just go along with it all and hope that things would improve. But how are things going to change, if you enable someone to keep doing what they are doing and do nothing or say nothing to help?

She then saw a stone on one of the shelves, and she asked, "What is this green stone? It seems to be talking to me?"

"It is an aventurine. It helps the person that it comes to or speaks to, to open themselves up to a world of opportunities and promotes career success."

She was amazed, because she said, "That is what I am working on in the moment!"

"I want you to keep it."

"No, I couldn't do that." she stated with some disappointment in her voice. "I couldn't just take it."

"Yes you can. It belongs to you."

She hesitated, but then she took it and held it close to her heart.

We went back out to the porch and the men got up to leave. Their energy had shifted. We said our fond farewells, and we all felt that what had just happened was as it should be.

13... No Dog Barking

Dreaming of a dog represents guidance, protection, and loyalty. The time has come when you need to act with the spirit of the dog — to defend your values or protect that which you hold sacred, and to be faithful, trustworthy and loyal for what you hold true.

While I was living at my healing center, my dog, Butch was my best buddy and companion. He was the best counselor/healer I ever met. He would greet my clients, enthusiastically, check them to make sure that they did not have a dog or any other animal hidden on their person or in their car or truck. Then he followed them into my healing room, got himself comfortable, and then proceeded to listen to them talk. When it came time for hands-on healing, he would get under the table and give energy to wherever it was needed the most. If they became emotional and started to cry, he would put his paws on the table to steady himself and then lick them to comfort them.

The morning he passed, I grieved, but knew it was his time to go. I did not have a client scheduled until 6:30 p.m. that evening. I thought maybe I should cancel and reschedule her one-hour appointment, but when I asked for guidance, I got "No, keep it." I thought that I probably would have grieved enough by then and that it would be good for me to help another and get back to my work. In any case, during the appointment I could focus my energies on my client, instead of on losing Butch.

My client showed up right on time, and when I went out to greet her, she asked, "Where's Butch?"

"He passed this morning," I said while trying to hold back tears.

She gave me her condolences as we went into the house. She wasn't a particularly spiritual person. I was counseling her through a bitter divorce, plus she was a former student of mine from my high school counseling days, when she first came to know and trust me.

Forty-five minutes into the session, she stopped, and said, "I can't go on with this session any longer until that dog outside your door stops barking!" I could not believe my ears!

"What dog?" I said.

She looked at me, as if I was crazy, and said, "You haven't heard the barking all this time?"

"What barking? I haven't heard any barking!"

As far as I was concerned it was silent outside. I then asked, "What does it sound like, this barking?"

She said, kind of timidly, "Well, it sounds like Butch's barking."

I jumped out of my chair, and in the same moment, so did she. I knew that Butch had died that morning, that his body was being cremated at the vet's, and that I would be picking up his ashes as soon as I could. We both flew to the front door, I thought maybe there was another dog at the door and I was so engrossed in the session that I just did not hear it barking. I opened the front door, but there was nothing there, and we both looked down and all around as far as the eye could see, and there was nothing!

She looked at me and said, "Maybe, the reason I was supposed to be here tonight was to let you know that Butch is still with you."

I said, "Maybe you're right." I smiled, we hugged and when she left, I realized that everyone and anyone can be "spiritual" in their own way.

For a long time I chose not to have any more pets because of my frequent traveling. A few years ago, dear friends from England, gifted me with a song called, "What's The Use of Wings?" Some of the lyrics talk about caging the ones we love the most. Is it because we are afraid to be alone? I thought back to all the years when I have never really been alone, and I decided that I needed to experience being truly alone, for the first time in my life, to see if I enjoy my own company. At first, it seemed lonely, but then I realized that I am never truly alone. As I traveled around the world and all over the U.S., I would love and take care of other peoples' pets and their homes. I recently decided to have another dog in my life. She is beautiful and very loving, coming to me from South Dakota. Her name is Ceallach (Gaelic) pronounced Kaylee, by my standards, and she loves to travel. She is a true blessing!

14... Parable of Mary and the Wren

Dreaming of a Wren suggests that we ask where in our lives do we need humility or cunning, or to glimpse the beauty of God /Goddess in all things, no matter how small.

On my birthday one year, I was presented with many gifts from friends and clients. My friend Pat gave me a three-foot tall statue of the Blessed Mother Mary.

This gift was significant because my deceased sister was Pat's grade school teacher and had given her a necklace with a picture of the Blessed Mother. The necklace had an image of Mary, created on a dark background from iridescent butterfly wings encased behind glass in an oval shape. She always cherished the necklace and was grateful to return the favor to me with the statue. Pat was raised in the same neighborhood as my family, but we did not become friends until we were older. She is presently an energy worker/holistic healer living in Florida.

When I have a place that I call home, I ask Spirit where to place things around the home. Since everything is energy, where you place things contributes to the energy of your home. I asked where to place the statue, and the answer was in the one corner of my healing room. In that room there were windows going across two walls, and she (the statue) was placed where the two walls of windows came together. I then had a friend/client do Feng Shui in my new place to keep the energy moving in order to maintain happiness, harmony, peace, and abundance. She noticed that the back part of the house was cut off and needed a continuous flow of energy. It happened to be my marriage corner, and it was next to my healing room. I asked how I could give that part of the house a continuous flow. She said, "Put something that has life in it in the far corner that is just opposite to the corner in the healing room." She suggested a wind ornament or a birdhouse to bring life and movement to create the energy needed.

I loved the idea of a birdhouse, so I proceeded to find one I liked. I asked my friend Jerome, who was in construction, to help me build a place for it. I found a handmade birdhouse at the local farmers' market. After talking to the man who made it, I felt that he loved what he was doing, and with that love, the birds would be attracted to it.

Jerome got a wooden pole, cut it to size and mounted the birdhouse directly across from the corner of my healing room. While I meditated each morning, I could see it from where I sat, and I could watch when the birds came to check it out. It was like watching to see who would be my new neighbors.

Each day a new winged one would appear, check out the birdhouse, then leave. It was always thrilling to see who was going to be next. Then one day a male wren hopped onto the perch, looked inside the entrance and went in. The reason I knew it was male was because the feathers were more intensely colored, which I learned from my bird book. It also said that male wrens do most of the nest building, and if the female liked the nest, she would stay.

So, I watched as the male wren took action in preparing the nest, and when he was done, he went on the roof of the birdhouse and waited for a female to inspect his work. Lo and behold, she appeared, sat on the perch and peeked inside. While this was happening the male puffed out his chest with pride. Then she left, and his chest deflated. He went inside the house to see his work and maybe improve upon it to attract her or another female again. Next he went back to the roof and waited. She returned, his chest puffed out again and he seemed to hold his breath. This time she went into the house, but as soon as he thought she would stay, out she flew, deflating his chest again. Once more, he inspected the nest and improved his work. Again, she returned. This time she went into the nest and out flew some twigs and grass, as if she were rearranging furniture. I watched the male on top of the roof as he was watching twigs flying out of the hole of the entrance. Once she seemed to have settled in, only then did he feel safe enough to venture into the birdhouse himself.

Of all the birds revered by the Druids, the wren was considered the most sacred. I always wondered why they would pick a nondescript little bird and not an obviously powerful bird like the eagle or hawk? There is a story from the western highlands of Scotland in which it was decided that the sovereignty of the feathered tribe should be given to the bird that could fly the highest. The favorite was naturally the eagle, who immediately began his flight toward the sun, fully confident in his ability to win the title, King of the Birds. When he found himself soaring high above his competitors, he proclaimed in a mighty voice his monarchy over all the winged ones. But suddenly, from under his wings popped the wren, which had hidden himself in the eagle's feathers. He flew a few inches higher and chirped out loudly, "Birds, look up and behold your King!"

In medieval Europe, especially among the lower classes, the wren was also considered the Virgin Mary's pet bird, while the ruling classes were often depicted as eagles, hawks, bears, etc., in stories and legends. After I read this particular fact, I looked toward the statue of the Blessed Mother and laughed, "So, you attracted the wrens to the birdhouse! How sweet! You wanted your favorite pet near you!"

We all came from tribes, and our ancestors knew that being in a tribe was important for their survival, and many tribes would travel long distances to escape the fury of Mother Nature or other tribes, just as the animals leave barren land and search for new food supplies. Our ancestors were not stupid; they knew that by watching the animals, insects, and birds, etc., their chances for survival would be better. When they traveled, their storytellers would be with them. They were very important to the tribe, because they were the teachers, and through stories the people learned many important lessons. These stories were parables, i.e., "narratives of imagined events used to illustrate moral or spiritual lessons."

When I tell the story of the wren hiding in eagle's wing, I also recognize that throughout history, in many different cultures, similar stories/tales have been told. Native Americans, for example, tell the same story, swapping a hummingbird for the wren. Why do you suppose these stories are almost identical, especially when there was no TV, Internet, Facebook, iPhones, etc.?

The tribes also had their *spiritual* teachers, the male/female shamans, priests, etc., whose dreams and visions helped the tribe with what they needed to learn. Most of the dreams and visions were told in story form. Since the shamans used the dreamtime for solutions to many problems or to ask the "Great Spirit" for a vision, they would tap into universal wisdom that anyone at any time can tap into, which is why, I believe, that there are similar stories from different cultures around our world. Even to this day, I believe, this tapping into the same pool of universal wisdom is how the same ideas come to different people in a dream or thought. As they had not heard or read the idea anywhere, they conclude that the idea is uniquely theirs and they get upset when someone else also implements it.

One of the reasons why I cannot take the Bible literally, is that to me it is a book of stories told and written down, at some time, to teach by illustrating in story form, a moral or spiritual lesson. I am sure some of the stories are based on true happenings or events, but again, stories repeated over time get lost in translation.

The wren allows us to glimpse the beauty of god/goddess in all things. That small bird is beautiful and never grandiose. With humility, gentleness and subtlety, it achieves self-realization. If, like the wren, we use cunning with humor and good intentions, we can also achieve much with little effort.

15... Through Unconditional Love

True partnership is achieved only by separate and whole beings who retain their separateness even as they unite. It signifies the gift of freedom from which flow all other gifts.

In my travels, I have come to realize that the entire world is sacred. I lived in Sedona, Ariz., and I heard from many people that this is a very spiritual and energetic place where people may have profound experiences. I have been many places on this beautiful Earth Mother, however, and I have had profound spiritual and energetic experiences whenever and wherever I needed to have them.

Once, for instance, on an island in the Caribbean, I was asked to work at a holistic center from mid-December to February. I left Pennsylvania the day after a Winter Solstice gathering I had at my healing center. It was freezing at the gathering the day before, and the next day I was transported to a tropical paradise.

The day I arrived at the holistic center, I was met by Jackie, the owner, a tall, thin, very attractive black woman originally from Brooklyn, N.Y. She built the place after several years of living on the property in a tent and supervising the construction. She had local natives working for her in various jobs such as cleaning, cooking, washing and massage work. She told me that not only would I be doing my work, but since I was living on the property, it was unexpected that my responsibilities also included helping the native staff with household chores. At first, I did not like the idea, but I soon pitched in without hesitation. I thought to myself, as I folded wash, wearing a bathing suit and sarong, looking out over the coral reef and beautiful blue green water "There can be no better place to fold wash!"

As I got acquainted with the staff, I fell in love with all of them, and I believe that they felt the same for me. On the very first day, I met the massage therapist, who was tall and thin, with high cheek bones and dreadlocks. The color of her skin was breathtaking, so black that it looked almost blue. I was later told that she was from the Maroon Tribe. When we met, she looked directly at me and said, "You have been here before."

"Yes, I have been to this island before."

With her eyes piercing my soul, she said, "No, you have been here before this lifetime!"

Her words went straight to the depths of me, and I shook from their intensity. She walked by me, and I just stood there in the wake of her energy.

I came to understand what it meant to be from the Maroon Tribe. Jackie gave me some information to read that said that when the African tribes were captured by the slave traders, they would take the whole tribe, kill off the shaman and transport them to the Caribbean Islands to break them for sale to Europe, and North or South America. The Maroon Tribe was the only tribe who could not be broken. Apparently, they had a surviving woman shaman who would create illusions that spooked the slave traders who told the tribe to go to the hills and leave them alone. Their independence is celebrated annually in the island hills with three days and nights of drumming and dancing.

One day, a woman showed up at the healing center for a week's stay. She was very uptight and stressed out, to the point of being hostile. I talked with her on several occasions to see if I could get to know her better. I came to understand that several of her past relationships wound up in court, where she always prevailed. She was defensive and hostile, unable to trust anyone. I told Jackie to be nice to her and to do what she wanted, or she might end up in court and probably lose. Jackie did not like the woman and wanted her to leave, but I convinced Jackie that that was exactly what she wanted Jackie to do. She listened and did what I said, but for most of the time she stayed hidden during the hostile woman's visit.

One morning, I noticed this woman alone after breakfast, looking out toward the ocean. I sat down by her and asked how she was enjoying her stay. She told me that it was OK so far, but that she did not like Jackie. She asked me about my work, and then she said that she had never had a good relationship with a man, that all men are stupid jerks, and that it was impossible to find an honest and loving man.

I told her about Adam, the man I met after Crow Woman told me the story of how she and I knew each other. In Crow Woman's story she mentioned a man named Moon Hawk and our love for each other. I wondered if he incarnated in this life and asked the Universe if he did and got 'yes'. I was excited and asked if I could meet him and if so, I would like to see who he was and maybe connect again.

One month later, a couple of friends asked if I wanted to go with them to enjoy a Native American Pow-Wow that was going on a short distance from where we lived. As we walked around we watched the American Indians playing drums and dancing. They announced that if anyone in the audience would like to dance, the Natives would choose the best woman dancer and jokingly she would win a date with one of the young braves. Yes, I won, but no, the young brave was not Moon Hawk. We laughed and walked around some more when a young man approached me. He had been sitting on a blanket with some of his friends watching the dance. He asked if he could talk with me and gave me his phone number, and said as he watched me dance, something happened to him, he felt a feeling deep within him that electrified him but also felt familiar. I must say that I did notice him sitting on the blanket with his friends earlier that day but also noticed how young he was. I told him that I would think about it and maybe I would call. He had big brown eyes behind dark rimmed glasses that were shy but pleading and said, "Please, I would love to talk to you."

A few days later, I did call, and he said that he made me a gift—a compilation of music on tape, and he wanted me to listen to it. He said that if I listened to his tape, I would get to know and understand him better. We met and went to dinner at his favorite restaurant, which was East Indian food. I love East Indian food and we truly had a wonderful evening and talked for hours. As he gave me the tape, he said I will call you tomorrow.

I listened to both sides of the tape, and realized that we also loved the same music! He had carefully chosen songs that were in my heart. I wondered how he could know? I could not believe that one of the songs was something I used to sing as a teenager. Adam was at least 20 years younger than me. Even though there was a huge age difference, when we were together we loved being with each other and completely forgot that there was any age difference. I soon grew to know that he was an old soul in a young body and one day after we made love, he looked at me and said, "We are more than just friends and lovers—we are kindred spirits." I was amazed he used that term and agreed, for by this time, I knew that the Universe had put us together again, and I got what I asked for when I asked to meet Moon Hawk, if he was in this lifetime. I was angry that he was younger, but I also knew that our relationship wasn't supposed to be long term – we both had different lives and different paths. He had already signed up to go off to the Peace Corps in a few months.

After telling the hostile woman this story, she seemed more relaxed and hopeful. The very next morning, I did my morning prayers and statements of gratitude out by the water's edge then walked over to see if the cook needed my help and ran into the woman, who was sitting peacefully yet had a look of astonishment on her face.

"Are you OK?" I asked.

"Was Adam, tall and thin with dark hair and wore dark rimmed glasses?"

"Yes," I answered, "How did you know that, since I did not tell you what he looked like?"

"This morning, as I was just coming out of a deep sleep, I was wondering about the story you told to me yesterday, and I asked myself if Adam was real. At that moment, just getting the sleep out of my eyes, I saw a tall, young dark-haired man standing in my room. He wore dark-rimmed glasses and said, 'Yes, I am Adam.' I quickly jumped up to see if he was actually in my room, and at that very moment, I saw you walk by my window. It was as if he turned to look at you, and then, as I saw you, he disappeared."

I could not believe what she was saying at first, but I knew that she wasn't making up this story. When I got back home from the Caribbean almost a month later, there, on my answering machine was a month old message from Adam, telling me that he was well and just thinking about me.

What I learned from this experience in love is that there is no separation when we cross from one lifetime to the next. But I also learned that having kindred spirits or being what some call "soul mates" does not always mean we are to spend each and every lifetime with them. Believe me, I love romance as much as anyone, but in new lifetimes we choose different lessons, and with them come different partners to help us learn. I do agree that in some lifetimes we choose to repeat the same lessons with the same partners, but our souls cannot expand and evolve if we keep relearning the same things with the same souls, especially if they have not evolved.

16...   The Cave

This is a symbolic depiction of the limited knowledge of the human condition in a world of mere likenesses and illusion; it is a person's task to escape this cave and ultimately attain a vision of the ideal world.

There were times when working at the holistic center on the island was challenging. Jackie was very afraid that she would lose what she had created, so sometimes she would get very paranoid around me and would accuse me of undermining her. It made her a bit crazy to have the locals like me, to see how well I managed things, how cooperative I was, and how easily I got along with different kinds of people. I would just look her right in the eyes and tell her that her mind was placing unreasonable fear in her and that I had no intention whatsoever of taking over. My experiences at previous places of employment primed me for this situation. Once I set my mind to something, I would do it well, causing some fearful people to assume the worst. I also reminded her that I wasn't in a management role so people could be more relaxed with me.

One day Jackie surprised me by inviting me to see a very sacred cave on the other side of the island. She knew that in my travels I had had many experiences, and that this would be something I would love. The arrangements were made, and we drove a long distance to meet a young native man, whom we found standing by his boat. He took us to a part of the island that very few nonlocals knew about, and Jackie informed me that no white person had ever experienced the place where we were going. The natives held that part of the island sacred, and since she had gotten to know me, she came to feel that I was someone whom she could trust, plus the word was around that the locals respected me.

The young man anchored the boat, grabbed his lantern, and we walked to the beach. We passed a short distance through some open fields of banana trees and sugar cane plants. My anticipation grew as we neared the cave entrance. I began to hear sounds coming from the cave opening, and I soon realized that the sounds were from countless bats screeching from the high ceiling.

"My Lady, please follow me," he said, leading the way with Jackie. We went through some narrow passages, and the light grew dimmer, but I could still see the bats flying around us. He turned on his lantern and asked politely whether he could guide me by holding my hand.

"Yes," I said. I wasn't afraid, but I was a little unnerved by all the bats flying about. I was thrilled to have this great opportunity to explore a very sacred place!

As we walked on, the cave passages got smaller and tighter, and all around us the bats flew and screeched. I kept reminding myself that they have sonar to help them maneuver about in the dark, so they probably would not fly into us. At times, we had to almost crawl our way through the passages. Not only could I hear bats swooshing by, but I could also hear running water. Our final destination was a small, low-ceilinged, grotto-like place. Our guide held the lantern high, indicating that we should sit on the larger rocks on the floor. I could feel the water around my feet as he guided me to my chosen rock, while Jackie chose a rock to the left of me. As our guide perched himself on the nearest rock, he held up the lantern to the far wall opposite to us, where I saw an amazing crystal altar jutting out from the wall. It was naturally carved by the water that dripped down the wall and ran onto the floor, between the rocks we were sitting on. It was so beautiful I could not believe my eyes, and I felt tremendous gratitude that I was here and able to see this natural beauty inside the Earth. We sat in awed silence.

I imagined that the natives had been coming here for hundreds of years, using it as a place to pray or make offerings to Mother Earth, but, all I really knew was that I felt grateful and humbled by it. This was my chance to experience what the ancients had experienced.

The guide broke the silence by asking me, "My Lady, the best way to experience this cave is in total darkness. Would you mind if I turned off my lantern?"

I hesitated, with bats still swooshing about, plus I knew that the darkness would be total, this far into the cave. I took a deep breath and said with a sigh, "Yes, I would like to experience this in total darkness."

At first I was nervous, not being able to see at all, but I told myself to relax and know that I was safe. As I relaxed, I opened and closed my eyes to see if there was any difference in the dark—there was none. I put my open hand up to my face and touched my nose with my palm, just to see if I could make out anything—nothing! It was that dark! In the darkness, I heard the bats swooshing about and the water running around me, and I somehow began to relax, and I felt comforted by this soft, warm and moist environment.

I wondered if this is how a baby feels being in the womb, for was this cave not a womb of Mother Earth? I do not know how long we were in total darkness, but with my eyes open, I began to see colors. At first, a quick flash, then, as I looked some more appeared. The colors varied and I saw swirls, waves and bursts, almost like looking at fireworks! I was enjoying the show immensely, and I wondered if the colors were somehow associated with the bats? I forgot about any and all fears.

Then, out of the darkness came the young man's concerned voice saying, "My Lady, are you all right?"

"Oh, yes, I am fine and truly enjoying the darkness!" I replied.

Then I explained to him and Jackie what I was seeing, and I asked about the colors. My question met with silence—they did not know. Then I remembered what I had read once, that shamans would go through ritualistic deaths. Most of the rituals were brutally hard on the body, mind and spirit, and the shamanic deaths enabled the initiate to put to rest the old ways of life and any identity. The initiates endured brutal tests of strength, psychic phenomena, and emotional instability. They were even spat upon and taunted to see if he or she could endure the duress with humility and fortitude. Ancient initiations were used to break down all their fears and preconceived ideas and allow them to be reborn without the former ego.

The shamanic symbol for death and rebirth is the bat, which hangs upside-down in a cave, like a newborn before it enters the world through its mother's womb. I also remembered reading that before you would become a healer or called a shaman, it was always preceded by a ritual death or death experience. I wondered, was Jesus Christ a Shaman? I recalled that the last part of an initiation for the would-be shamans was to spend time in open graves or caves, covered over by blankets. This ceremony took them out of their natural environment, and out of their conscious minds, which made them go within themselves, just like a grave or cave takes you beneath the surface of the Earth, and all this transformation was done without any chemical inducement. Not that I'm comparing this to the duress experienced by Shaman initiates, but I was still struck that here I was, seeing colors inside a totally dark cave. I couldn't help but wonder what visions they might experience while being completely buried. What I knew was that all my preconceived ideas and fears were gone. Was I being shown my own transformation from within, my own internal creative nature, or was I in a waking dream?

I heard the young man say, "I believe we need to turn the lantern back on, and I will do it slowly, so our eyes do not hurt."

I was a little disappointed, for I was taken by the colors and really did not want to come back from the beauty I was seeing in the darkness, but I agreed.

After my cave experience, I was struck by Plato's "The Allegory of the Cave" where people are tied to their seats and they spend their lives staring at a wall in front of them. Behind them is a fire that casts shadows on the wall. To them, the shadows are real. The following is an excerpt:

> Socrates said, "And now look again, and see what will naturally follow if the prisoners are released and disabused of their error. At first, when any of them is liberated and compelled suddenly to stand up and turn his neck round and walk and look towards the light, he will suffer sharp pains; the glare will distress him, and he will be unable to see the realities of which in his former state he had seen the shadows; and then conceive someone saying to him that what he saw before was an illusion, but that now, when he is approaching nearer to being, and his eye is turned towards more real existence, he has a clearer vision – what will be his reply? And you may further imagine that his instructor is pointing to the objects as they pass and requiring him to name them – will he not be perplexed? Will he not

fancy that the shadows which he formerly saw are truer than the objects which are now shown to him?

"The entire allegory, I said, you may now append, to the previous argument; the prison-house is the world of sight, the light of the fire is the sun, and you will not misapprehend me if you interpret the journey upwards to be the ascent of the soul into the intellectual world according to my poor belief, which, at your desire, I have expressed, whether rightly or wrongly, God knows. But, whether true or false, my opinion is that in the world of knowledge the idea of good appears last of all, and is seen only with an effort; and, when seen, is also inferred to be the universal author of all things beautiful and right, parent of light and of the lord of light in this visible world, and the immediate source of reason and truth in the intellectual; and that this is the power upon which he who would act rationally, either in public or private life, must have his eye fixed.

"Better to be the poor servant of a poor master, and to endure anything, rather than think as they do and live after their manner?"

I looked around me, and I noticed Jackie looking back at me with a peaceful smile. The guide said, "Let us go to the cleansing waters!" He put his hand out for me to take, helped me up, and guided us to a different part of the cave. I felt joy and peace at the same time! There was another opening with a stream of running water, but this water was much faster and had a stronger current. Its height was about a foot or so, again rushing around rocks on the floor. I followed them by lying down and holding onto the rocks around me. The water flowed rapidly all over our bodies, and it wasn't easy at times to hold onto the rocks, but I did. It was refreshing. Then it was time to leave this magical cave, but not before Jackie wanted to show me another miraculous wonder inside the cave.

There are "blue holes" around the island, which are beautiful sky-blue pools of water that are always blue and not from a reflection of the sky. These pools are so deep that not even scuba divers have been able to find their bottoms, and the blue is caused by phosphorescent, living creatures that inhabit these holes. There it was, a "blue hole" in the darkness of the cave, and when the guide held the lantern up to shine on the water, it was a beautiful sky blue!

He and Jackie asked if I cared to take a swim, but I decided that my fear of not being a good enough swimmer and the thought that it was considered bottomless, did not make for an inviting venture.

They decided that it was getting late and we should just go. It took a while to return to the cave entrance, and I realized that the sun had set, and that we were looking up at a beautiful star-lit sky. On the ride home, we talked about many things—our theories, our feelings, and our joys. I felt that we had bonded in a new way.Here is another excerpt from Socrates in Plato's *The Allegory of the Cave*.

> "Anyone who has common sense will remember that the bewilderments of the eyes are of two kinds, and arise from two causes, either from coming out of the light or from going into the light, which is true of the mind's eye, quite as much as of the bodily eye; and he who remembers this when he sees anyone whose vision is perplexed and weak, will not be too ready to laugh; he will first ask whether that soul of man has come out of the brighter light, and is unable to see because unaccustomed to the dark, or having turned from darkness to the day is dazzled by excess of light. And he will count the one happy in his condition and state of being, and he will pity the other; or, if he have a mind to laugh at the soul which comes from below into the light, there will be more reason in this than in the laugh which greets him who returns from above out of the light into the cave."

These parts of Plato's work best express my feelings and thoughts from my own cave experience. I do encourage you to read his work for your own expressions and thoughts.

My transformation from my cave experience was the opportunity to know simply that in the darkness there is light!

17... Good Friend Audean

Otter represents joy, play, and helpfulness. It invites us to play, "to go with the flow" of life and experience, and to become a child again. When I dream of a good friend, I can see where I am being my own good friend, to play and be a child again.

I met Audean when she presented her artwork at a spiritual workshop. After her presentation, I went up to her and said that I could see angels in her artwork, even though there was not a single angel visible to her eyes. She thanked me, and thus began a long and wonderful friendship. Over the years, we often talked, because she, at times, was the only person in my life who spoke my language and understood what I was saying and experiencing on my spiritual journey. This has made me realize that the angels I saw in her paintings, all those years ago, were what she would come to represent in my life—an Earth angel on my path to help support me emotionally and spiritually, as I would be for her. Audean is a spectacular artist who has lived, worked, and raised a family in New York City for over 30 years. She has had many spiritual experiences, such as the following story that she told me long ago, that I now share with you with her permission.

One Sunday night Audean was finishing up some illustrations for a children's book that needed to be delivered on Monday morning at 9:00 a.m. She lived at 94th & West End Avenue, and she had to be at 51st & 3rd Avenue. She had also made an appointment to go to Columbia Presbyterian Hospital at 168th and Broadway at 10:00 a.m. The problem was that a transit strike was scheduled for Monday morning, which meant that the buses and subways would not be in operation, and she thought to herself, "How in the world am I going to get to the East Side from the Upper West Side in that short amount of time?"

When Monday morning arrived, she looked out the window to see bumper-to-bumper cars and hundreds of people walking to work. As she was looking at the scene below, she said, "OK, God, I am going to 51st & 3rd Avenue and then 168th & Broadway, and the rest is up to you!"

She had no idea how this would be accomplished or what to do. All dressed up with her portfolio under her arm, she thought she would go to 96th & Broadway to thumb a ride with someone, but when she got there, the traffic was backed up in every direction, and all the cars were filled with people—no one seemed likely to pick her up. In fact, there were about 80 people on the corner around her, thinking the same thing. So, she walked half way up the block to get away from the crowd, when she saw a middle-aged white-haired man in a white raincoat making his way through the crowd, looking right at her. As he proceeded in her direction, still gazing at her, she could not help but stare back. He walked right up to her and said, "Are you going down town?"

"Yes!"

"Follow me," and she did. They walked across Broadway and down to 96th St., where his big white Cadillac was parked. He opened the door and said, "Get in, please." He then went around to the driver's side and got in. This was such an unusual happening that she was very quiet, and as he proceeded to start the car, she noticed as he pulled out of the parking space that 96th St. was so empty that he was able to make a U-turn to go East. There was literally no traffic! So, he drove over to Central Park and inquired about her destination. She told him her destination.

"Oh, good!" he said. "I have to meet someone a block from there."

"That is convenient. Where do you work?"

"On Wall Street," he said without volunteering any other information.

He drove her to her destination without issue. She arrived 15 minutes early at the publishing company and delivered her work to the Art Director on the 9th floor. When she came back down to the street, it was bumper to bumper again, and she thought, "I'll never get a ride, so I'll walk." She then walked across town through Central Park to 8th Ave. When she got to 55th St., she asked, "OK, God, what do I do now?"

Just then, in the middle of all that traffic, a man hanging out of a window in an old brown van yelled, "168th St., $5.00!"

She leapt off the curve and said, "Here, wait for me!"

He got out and opened the back door of the van, where she saw some rolled-up old rugs and several people sitting, all dressed up for work. They drove all the way up town and he dropped her off at 168th St. for her appointment at the hospital at 10:00 a.m.

When she finished with her appointment, she walked to Broadway and 168th St., where the traffic was still terrible and hundreds of people were milling about. Just then a bus pulled right up and stopped at the curb. She thought, "A bus? There are no buses running!"

The doors opened, and some people got out, and she called to the driver, "What kind of bus is this?"

"This is a New York University bus for faculty members. You look like a teacher. Get in!"

Very surprised, she got onto the bus, and the driver proceeded to drive down Broadway to 96th, where she got off, just two blocks from home!

"Thank you, thank you, thank you, God!" she said, laughing. It wasn't until much later that she realized that the man in the white raincoat was truly an angel and the rest of the people? Just Earth Angels helping other people perhaps.

I often wondered why certain places on this planet are more creative and successful then others, and other places, no matter how often things change, are never creative or successful. I always go back to the science of it all, and I know that everything is made up of energy, and whatever energies come together will make it one or the other. When I first discovered that New York City sits on a slab of granite, I thought, that is definitely a strong and solid foundation to build upon. I found out that the spiritual properties of granite encourage us to go with the flow and help us to find our highest path. Maybe that is why most people who go or live in New York City are driven to do their best, and use their creativity to become very successful. Unfortunately, the influence can go either way, meaning that some people may be driven to be creatively successful at their worst!

Angel Fire, N.M., is another place where I experienced Earth energies that help to create what we believe, thus manifesting success or failure.

When I left my healing center and drove west with only what I could fit into my little blue car, I ended up in Eagle Nest, N.M. I rented a place by the lake for six months and then lived in Angel

Fire, both of which are located on the Enchanted Circle. I felt that I had come home, especially in Angel Fire. Why? This place would help me to manifest instantly whatever I thought or dreamt. It would just come to me. Since energy is always moving, the only time I've felt it stop was when I had a block or fear, which meant I was living from my head and not my heart. Angel Fire made me feel at home, and "home is where the heart is."

In my opinion, in order to be in sync, in tune or in harmony with the Universe—and the Universe is the place where there is unlimited creative potential—we need to be in a good place, surrounded by people, where the creative energies will help us feel unlimited.

Taos, N.M., where the Enchanted Circle supposedly began, is about a 30-minute drive from Angel Fire, but initially I never wanted to live in Taos because most of the people there believed that "The Taos Mountain (which the Enchanted Circle went around) would either welcome you or chew you up and then spit you out!" which is why, they explained, that the energies there were very difficult for most people to survive. There were even jokes like, "If you want to make a million dollars in Taos, come with two million." I could not believe what I was hearing. I would answer them by saying, "Why would any part of Mother Earth chew me up and then spit me out, if I was a child of the Earth?" and, "If my human body is made up of Earth energies, how could she reject me?" On the other hand, I have seen too often how people create struggle for themselves to survive.

"I've struggled but I am still here!" some would claim, as if it were a badge of honor to struggle! Or others would just sheepishly leave. Audean could have struggles the day of the transit strike, but instead she set her intent and allowed miracles to unfold.

I knew that when I eventually did live in Taos, there would be something for me to learn, or I would not have been drawn there. And that came true. I did meet many great and wonderful people while living in Taos. I watched, observed and learned, and I am very grateful for the experiences!

In Glastonbury, England, spiritual people also claim that no one who comes there can make any money, and that survival there is very difficult. I did not feed into their beliefs, and in time I did workshops there on the energies and beliefs surrounding money.

What I learned from Taos and Glastonbury is that I had some unconscious negative beliefs around the energy of money, and that the people along my path had been mirroring back to me what I believed, even though on a conscious level, I denied those beliefs or claimed that I had worked through them all. Some people believe that one needs to struggle in order to survive, and that struggling somehow gives us a feeling of achievement. Now, however, I feel accomplished when I learn from whomever or whatever is on my path. I gave the workshops on the energies and beliefs surrounding money in order to remind and convince myself of these things that I have come to know.

18...   Extraterrestrials

Symbolically, extraterrestrials, "aliens," etc., whenever or however they show up in your dream state, represent something foreign to you; the consciousness you are experiencing is foreign to you.

I knew a woman named Connie, who was interested in furthering her spiritual growth. She and her then boyfriend, but now-husband, went through the AA 12-Step Program, and she experienced some flashbacks of some childhood traumas. She realized that when her father used to come home drunk and beat her, she would dissociate and think of herself at the playground. Then, if she ended up in the hospital, she would just think that it all happened while playing with her friends. The only thing that scared her was the occasional flashback associated with "alien abductions." She kept seeing herself being probed and analyzed, while seeing "alien" beings around her.

At first, we did some regressions and then soul-retrieval work, which is the process of bringing back fragments of our essence that have dissociated, due to traumas. She was still frightened of being abducted again. After the soul-retrieval work, she came to realize that she had allowed the abductions in a contract she had made before she came to be in this lifetime, and that it was part of her earth's journey to help "alien" friends observe earthling progress.

One day she suggested that we would meditate together, get ourselves into a higher frequency, and contact these beings. At first, it went slowly and nothing happened, then she felt a presence that felt very heavy for her. She was sitting next to me on the floor, and she asked me to see if I could hold the energy. I gave it a try, and I was able to hold the energy in the room. I was then transported to another time.

I found myself sitting on the floor of a huge room with many chairs that surrounded a large, oblong table. In the chairs were various beings of many different shapes, sizes and colors, wearing elaborate apparel. They were all listening to an immense reptilian-looking being, who stood at the head of the table. I found out later that his name was Zetar. He had a long face, with large eyes on either side of his head and very scaly skin, and he was wearing some sort of garment that looked like armor. His presence was enormous and foreboding. Looking more closely, I saw no noticeable ears, and his mouth was large, with sharp, protruding teeth. I must say I was a little scared, but not totally frightened. As I observed my surroundings, it was obvious to me that I had been transported to a galactic counsel of sorts. All at once, Zetar stopped, and glanced at me. He seemed angry and annoyed, and I realized that I must have become visible to him and all who were present.

He glared at me, saying, "How is this human here? Who are you? Human energy is too low to be present here!"

I did not know what to say, and then I became frightened. As he stared and scowled at me, his large eyes started to recognize something in me.

"You are the Red Goddess, and I am honored that you are present at our counsel!"

In Hindu tradition, Red Goddess means "Light of Manifestation." Her name is Lalita Tripurasundari, where Lalita means "She Who Plays." All of creation, manifestation and dissolution are considered to be a play of the goddess. Tripura is a metaphor for a human being.

Zetar then turned to the others and began to tell them how he knew me. Apparently, I am widely known as a wayfarer – one who has totally committed, without question, to go, when asked by a higher power, wherever he/she is needed the most. He then said that we had met when I was serving in a much older universe. This information, of course, was all new to me. I did not even think that such encounters were possible, but yet it was happening.

A few years earlier, by the way, I was coming home late from a meditation group, driving alone on a back-country road, and I noticed bright lights swirling around me. At first, I thought it was a police car, but, when I looked in my rearview mirror, there was no car behind me. As I looked up, I saw hovering overhead multi-colored lights on what looked like some sort of spacecraft. I thought my eyes were playing tricks on me because it was late and I was tired, but the lights would not go away. I was excited and scared all at once! As I was trying to keep the car on the road, I looked up and kept saying, "Don't beam me up! Love and Light! Love and Light!"

I don't know why, but I felt at the time that this would help me. I looked at the clock in the car to make sure I wasn't losing any time, and then I looked back at the craft. It was beautiful, kind of mushroom-shaped against the dark sky, with lights swirling around the bottom of it. When I got to an open road with more light, the craft disappeared. I then drove the rest of the way home and pulled into my driveway, where I began to doubt myself. I got out and gazed at the star-filled sky, and I noticed a very bright light in the distance and asked myself, "Did I really see what I saw?" At that very moment, as if it had heard me, the bright light shot straight up into the starry sky and disappeared. I did not doubt myself again.

Returning to my appearance before the counsel, I asked Zetar if he knew that most humans think that the reptilian race is a negative force in the universe and that Reptilians have some connection with what is known as the Illuminati.

"Yes, I know that, and I know how foolish this concept is. We Reptilians are not stupid, but yes, there may be a few of us who think we are better than most and would like to destroy others. Most Reptilians, like most other intelligent beings throughout the Universe, are in service to a Higher Source. If we were as ignorant and arrogant as to destroy the Earthlings and/or the Earth, it would be harmful to the whole universe. Just because we don't understand whole civilizations does not mean that we should destroy them! It is like having a diseased foot – do we cut it off, or do we try to heal it, so it can benefit the whole? The reason we are holding this counsel is to help the Earth on many levels, so we all can benefit from its healing. We consider the Earth to be a very primitive part of the Universe, but it is also a very beautiful planet, in our eyes."

When I heard this, truth resonated within me. I remembered a vision I had received long before, when I asked Spirit to give me a mental picture of the future, and I saw geese flying in a "V" formation. I realized that the geese can teach us what humans need to know. In order to get to where we need to be on a higher level—both individually and collectively—we never have just one true leader. One moves to the front in order to lead only at the moment when one is strong enough to lead without ego, without obstructing others' views, and when one is able to guide and help the trailing ones, making it easier for them to follow. Such a temporary leader knows when it is time to fall back and graciously receive another's lead, so we all can keep flying.

The "V" formation is the symbol for the sacred feminine that holds the energy to be open to all possibilities. I then felt relieved, but I also felt that we have misjudged these Reptilian beings. Is it because we fear their strength and appearance, or is it just because we need to blame others for our own insecurities? In deference to their gentle nature, I put quotation marks around my use of the word "alien," for, although their appearance is different, they seem to know love and care for us. I have been more frightened by some humans.

In Shamanism, when others come into our space and surroundings, we honor their presence because we know that it is god/goddess manifested in a form that is telling us what we need to know in that moment.

For example, when ants come into my house and seem to disturb my surroundings, I know that Spirit is telling me where I need to practice teamwork and patience. Once I get the message, the ants will leave on their own accord, without me trying to destroy them. Doesn't this happen in many ways, for aren't we all part of the Great Mystery, and aren't we all messengers for each other?

19... Shamanism & Crystals

Crystals have been used for centuries, and they symbolize reflection of light, the light of God, clarity and purity. They were used to promote health, good fortune, predict the future, enhance energies, and, at times, to make magic. Shamans used them for healing and rituals. Even today crystals are used in technology to produce energy.

For years, I have been fascinated with crystals, gems, jewelry, etc. I would go to rock & gem shows to talk to collectors and rock hounds and listen to their stories about how they got started or where they would trek to dig for crystals.

I also studied books on crystals to find out why I was attracted to a particular gem at a particular time, and it would always amaze me that what I was going through at the time was exactly the energy I needed from the crystal I purchased!

I decided to journey into the crystal realm one day to see what I could discover. I went to my favorite sacred oak tree, and I visualized myself descending to the inner Earth. I came to a realm where there were thousands of spirit beings concentrating their skills on certain areas to form crystal clusters. What was even more amazing was that the spirit beings were also crystals that moved and worked their wonders to help create crystals. I moved among them, feeling a sense of welcoming joy. I watched and observed the amethyst-crystal beings working to form amethysts, the citrine-crystal beings to form citrine, and so on. Also, other clusters of these spirit beings were creating, from combinations of crystals already formed and other minerals in the earth, new formations of gems and minerals.

As I was observing and enjoying it all, a kind of parade of crystal beings came toward me. I realized that the crystal beings approaching me were some sort of royalty that had come to welcome my presence among them. Since I loved crystals so much, they were pleased that I was moved to visit their realm. It was strange, but yet familiar all at once. I felt that I was visiting a totally different planet instead of the inner Earth! I wondered whether, when the Earth was being formed, these beings came from another place and time to help create in our world what they knew from theirs.

I know we are multi-dimensional beings, living on many levels of existence, but our minds do not easily comprehend this, because we limit ourselves with our thoughts and fears. We would rather catalog everything, label it, and store it, and then feel complacent. But what if the statement, "We are All Children of God and Children of Mother Earth," is true?" Wouldn't that mean that we can do everything we can imagine, plus what is beyond our imaginations? Since I am the daughter of my biological parents, wouldn't it follow that I can do everything they could do and even better, and with my own uniqueness, do things that are totally different from them? Jesus once said, "All this you can do, and more." Wasn't He considered the Son of God and aren't we all sons and daughters of god/goddess? All of us limit our own potentials with our limited thoughts, so we can continue being complacent in this limited-thinking world.

As the parade of crystal beings approached me, I felt a sense of hierarchy among them. Two beings with seemingly higher status then the rest handed me a bolt of material made of woven crystals. It felt soft and bumpy, and it sparkled! I then wondered how this place was illuminated, and from where, for there was no Sun or view of the sky. It was more like a space that had some structure to it. Four of the beings wrapped the bolt of material around me, covering me from neck to ankles with long sleeves. It felt soft and lightweight against my body. I knew that they were gifting me with an appropriate garment for this realm. I heard words in my head that told me that they enjoyed making this gift for me and that it was mine every time I come to visit. I was then, and remain to this day, very grateful.

When I looked more closely at the garment, I saw that it was like wearing a web, woven together with strands of glistening threads made from crystals and faceted gems. How on Earth did they create this miracle fabric? Was I wearing Indra's Net?[1]

Everything is energy vibrating at various frequencies. Like fire, water, earth and air, even if we could not see them, we would feel their presence. When all these energies come together, they form completely different frequencies, and, over time, these frequencies develop into flowers, trees, animals, insects, fish, etc. So why couldn't different frequencies from different parts of the universe come together to create something totally different here on Earth? Maybe there are "aliens" among us who need different areas on this planet to live, bringing with them their own unique talents to form this unique and beautiful planet we call our home.

I then remembered what Liza told me when she gave me the smaller sketch portrait of my higher self. In her portrait of me, she

---

1. My mentor, Michael Elia, who has encouraged me to write, recently told me of Indra's Net, after I read my story to him. He told me that I needed to look it up, so after I Googled it and read what it meant in ancient Hinduism, and physics, I sat dumbfounded for a long time.

drew crystals above and around my head and explained that they represented people whom I would meet along my journey. She said that they would be like precious gems that I would gather together and form into a network. She also told me that I was an energy weaver. Indra's Net explains that there are multi-faceted crystals at each cross point of the crystal strands that reflect the others, and if there was a mark or flaw on one of the crystals, all the others would have the same mark or flaw. It also shows that the structure of the entire universe is made of interconnecting crystal strands.

When I mentioned crystal strands to another friend, she said, "I cannot imagine how that could be."

"Isn't everything made out of Light, and maybe these strands that make up our universe and the interconnections between us are simply strands of light?"

I told her that a shaman once told me that if you ask a shaman what enlightenment means, he or she will simply tell you that it is simply the ability to see into the darkness. What if enlightenment, or our ability to see into the darkness, comes from our own light that shines within all of us? Don't we say that children are closest to the Light of God, and that we need to be childlike to go to God? Children keep their lights on when they transition into this world, and all we have to do is allow them to keep them on and turn our own lights back on.

20... Consciousness

Seeking after wholeness is the Spiritual Warrior's quest. And yet what you are striving to become in actuality is what, by nature, you already are. Become conscious of your essence and bring it into form, then express it in a creative way.
—The Book of Runes

Consider the following phrases: *Christ consciousness...take the middle road...simply be awake...be in the moment...re-member who I AM,...just be*, etc. I have come to believe from my journey that staying awake, being in the moment, Christ Consciousness, and being Godlike are all the same idea – just in different words. When we are truly conscious, we are simply awake to everything around us. Paying attention to our dreams and whatever we receive in meditations will help us to stay awake.

I have read that in ancient times another word for shaman was augur. These people were trained to interpret signs from nature, particularly with birds. They knew that we are one with all things and that by being in the moment, we are being instructed and talked to every moment by what they believed were their gods/goddesses. They even had colleges or schools of higher learning, whose best graduates were given employment by the regional hierarchy to help the whole community with their knowledge of architecture, art, politics and personal empowerment.

The word "inauguration" derives from augur, which means that we, in our own nation, can pay attention to the signs around us, whether in nature or in the processes by which we choose our politicians or celebrities. I believe that all of us today can be modern-day augurs and shamans, if we just stay in the moment and pay attention to what nature is telling us. It is not fortune telling, because what we witness in the moment allows us to change our minds now, so as to change our future. The first commandment tells us to be aware of what false gods/goddesses we put before us. When this was written, they talked about idols in the sense of pagan statues. Today we could substitute TV, money, technology or any other strictly material item of any kind for modern-day idol that takes us away from our spirituality. Should we not worship the god/goddess within all of us, for isn't our true nature being natural, and therefore, being who we truly are. And, don't we find our true nature by listening to our inner voice and the voices of Nature? Isn't god/goddess in all things? If we would focus on our own paths and not compare ourselves to others, wouldn't this world be less competitive, greedy, spoiled and judgmental?

I have come to realize that I was led to shamanism so I could learn to pay more attention to Nature. By paying attention to Nature, I was led to be in the moment, and when I remained in the moment, I could stay awake and aware by observing what comes on my path. All of this led me to explore augury. One of the books that I read that I really resonated with, was *Secret Language of Birds: A Treasury of Myths, Folklore and Inspirational True Stories* by Adele Nozedau. It was one of those books that you know you were *led* to for a distinct purpose. I felt the same feeling when I read Barbara Marciniak's *Bringers of the Dawn* and *Return of the Bird Tribe* by Ken Carey.

The word augur is relatively new for me, even though I have been associated with birds for many years. My name Arael means

Spirit of the Birds, or Angel of the Birds, I did not know this when the name was given to me. I have come to understand that this ancient knowledge has been in my DNA and lineage for 3,000 years, and all I have to do is ask for that door to be opened. It is like opening the zipper to the pocket of knowledge already in my purse that I have carried around with me since being in the womb. This auguring tool helps me to enjoy life and make it easier. Not only have I been able to interpret signs from birds, but also from all other living creatures that come onto my path, for I know that all life is sacred.

The sight of a bird flying or some other form of life passing awakens in me a pocket of knowledge of spiritual concentration that prompts a swift grasp of things, sometimes as a forewarning and other times showing me that I am on the right path. Dr. Maya Angelou wrote years ago that "we are all creatures under God's watchful eye, we stumble and fumble and fall but we are equipped to fly...."

Staying in the moment, is not easy, because we become unaware when we think in the past and become anxious when we think about the future. So it is essential to practice being in the moment! I have been practicing for years, and I still have some difficulty staying in each moment, but it is getting easier!

Many years ago I was given a poster that read...

"I was sitting regretting the past and fearing the future. Then God spoke to me, and I listened. He said, 'When you live in the past with its guilt and regrets, it is hard, for I AM not there, my name is not I WAS. When you live in the future with its anxieties and fears, it is hard, for I AM not there, my name is not I WILL BE, but when you live in the present, it is easy, for I AM here, my name is I AM."
                    – Anonymous

I would sit under the framed poster every day to meditate and pray until about 13 years ago, when I gave the poster to someone who I thought could use it more than me. This poster continually reminded me that it is hard to live in the past or future in my thoughts, which bring on emotions, because my true power is in the moment, where I AM clear from all emotions and thoughts, and where I can go to the inner place of peace, which is the Divine. Today, I observe my life as if I am watching a rose open, petal by petal. I see the beauty of it, and I know that it is important for my future for me to observe the NOW, so I can make better conscious choices for a more conscious world – my world – whether it be my immediate world or the world as a whole.

While I am in the moment, I can clearly observe who I draw to myself, whether lover or friend, and they are but a reflection, in that moment, of what I like or dislike, and/or love or don't love about myself.

Another important step for was remembering my dreams. By practicing and seeing the symbols as messages from my insight, I found that I could be consciously aware of what I needed to do to change my mind, so I can in turn change my world.

My dreams give me insight as to where I AM on a conscious level and what I need to change or not change within myself. I trust what I receive in my dreams because I believe that in the unconscious we do not lie to ourselves by rationalizing or talking ourselves into or out of something.

I teach others to see and be honest with themselves.

I have chosen not to own anything in the last 20 years, except the car I drive, because things may own me. By doing this, I have discovered that whatever I need – whether it is a house to live in or food to eat – will just come to me when and where I need it. For instance, when I went west, I did not know anyone, I just filled my little car with what I needed in the moment and went west until I felt I was in the right place. Just before I ran out of money, I met a woman who was a professional house sitter, and we became fast friends. When she got more houses to sit than she could accommodate, she gave me the name of the person to contact, which started me on the adventure of house sitting, pet sitting or plant sitting.

One time I was house sitting and secure in a place for a month, but I didn't have any other clients at the moment so I was trying to stretch my money. Within that month I ran out of food, so as I was opening my last can of soup, I said to myself, "I guess tomorrow I will start a fast. I have a beautiful place to live, I have gas in my car, and I have all that I need for the next two weeks to live comfortably, so I will just fast until I can have food."

Within minutes of this statement to myself, there came a knock on the door. When I opened it, the man I was dating at the time was standing there with both arms filled with groceries.

"I was grocery shopping for myself," he said, "and as I was standing in line I picked up a calendar with pictures of animals and birds, and the animals told me that you needed food. I took my groceries out to my car and went back in the store and asked to be guided to what you might need, and here I am!"

"Oh, my, you really didn't have to do this. I had just decided to go on a fast."

I could not believe what I was seeing or hearing, and I felt a little embarrassed that he had spent his money to buy me groceries.

"When you learn how to graciously receive," he said, "maybe then you will not have to learn to receive."

He was absolutely right and once again, I was very grateful, and I knew this was my lesson at that time.

Recently, I decided to be open to owning some things for a while, because I do not fear anymore that they will own me. By being in the moment, I will know whether to let it go or pass it on.

Why do I use god/goddess to express myself at times? Because I know, as our ancestors knew, that we cannot have one gender without the other. Even in nature, we see that in order to have a population, we need both male and female. To me, Goddess represents the Mother (Divine Feminine) and God represents the Father (Divine Masculine). Both energies are within each of us. When we create our reality from our hearts and our Inner Voice, we listen, being open to receive, then we take action by physically bringing into manifestation something new or old, depending on what is in our hearts, in that moment.

Feminine energies are about nurturing, nourishment, abundance, loving myself, caring about what is good for me, which also reflects others, and observing and paying attention to what feels right. Aren't all these traits considered being a good mother? Male energies are about physically creating what my heart desires, taking action to create, doing what needs to be done whether it be feeding myself, providing shelter, food, or money, so I can follow my heart's desires.

What we sometimes forget, however, is that all the while we need to remember to take care of ourselves, so that we can be sure we have the strength to be able to take care of others.

The trouble with most of us is that the fear of dying, starving, being homeless, etc., is so strong that we don't take the time to listen to what is really best for us and those around us. We think that we know, and we act accordingly, but most of the time our choices are not healthy for us, nor do they create happiness. So we must listen to the advice from our Mother, the Divine Feminine, in the moment, which will help us create Heaven on Earth. then we need to enlist the Divine Masculine to make it happen. Thus we create what is best for us at that moment.

Ancient people knew that Mother Earth gives us what we need, and she gives abundantly! The only difference is that most humans today don't respect her enough to give back and not deplete her. We know that if we keep taking, one day she will die, and then we and our children will die. Listen to the birds, trees, insects, fish and all there is that surrounds us and know that they support us on our journeys. It is not what we think but what we know, in the moment!

When I hear people say that we need rain, we need snow, we need, etc. I simply say that that is what you think is needed and that Mother Earth already knows what is needed. If things aren't working for you now, then you need to change or move. We humans do not like changing or moving, but didn't our ancestors figure that one out a long time ago? They had the courage to seek out new places and have new adventures. Are we simply so stuck in our ways that we want the world to change instead of ourselves? Are we so afraid of change that we would rather complain about our lives instead of taking action to improve them? It takes courage to make changes, but didn't our ancestors show us that in order to survive and be happy, we need to pay attention to our environment and to who and what is surrounding us?

Trying to control the weather/environment, will have consequences. We are interfering with Mother Earth and her path: "The road to Hell is paved with good intentions." I always wondered what that quote really meant until the day I was working with my Peruvian shaman teacher and he said, "There are no sins, and if there were any, it would be to interfere on anyone's path." He explained, "When you think you know what is best for someone or something and have 'good intentions' and do so or tell them so, you interfere with what they need to come to, on their own. How else will they learn to take responsibility for their actions? Maybe, they need to experience the consequences to learn what was important for them to learn."

If we could be content with what is, then what a concept – we might be content!

I am not saying that I disapprove of progress, I am all for it! I just mean that if we intend to create "new and improved" to better our lives, why not look at the whole picture – like the eagles and hawks, they go to a higher viewpoint, look at the whole picture, see what is best and then take action to nourish themselves.

In my life, the choices that have been best for me and those around me were those for which I took the time to slow down, focus on the choices, get as much information as I could—including signs, symbols, dreams—then determine what felt right in the moment and then take action.

I then use my divine feminine and divine masculine to create what is truly important in my life. Yes, others around me question my choices, but I know that no matter what it looks like to others, it is simply right for me.

Remember the phenomenal quote from Marianne Williamson, *"Our deepest fear is not that we are inadequate. Our deepest fear is that we are powerful beyond measure. It is our light, not our darkness that most frightens us. We ask ourselves, 'Who am I to be brilliant, gorgeous, talented, fabulous?' Actually, who are you not to be? You are a child of God. Your playing small does not serve the world. There is nothing enlightened about shrinking so that other people won't feel insecure around you. We are all meant to shine, as children do. We were born to make manifest the glory of God that is within us. It's not just in some of us; it's in everyone. And as we let our own light shine, we unconsciously give other people permission to do the same. As we are liberated from our own fear, our presence automatically liberates others."* [1]

Another important quote: *"We dance around a ring and suppose, when the secret sits in the middle that already knows."* -Anonymous

Are there really secrets? No. When someone calls something a secret or their secret, they just want to own it, claim it and use it for themselves. They think that they have something only they know, which gives them some benefit over others. What a joke! Why? Because, if we really wanted to know something, all we have to do is ask, and the answer will come to us. "The truth will be revealed." OK, you are saying, what if we don't know the question? "No problem!" as our Jamaican friends say so eloquently. When we stop asking, it means that we really don't want to know. There is a funny scene in the movie "Bruce Almighty" where Jim Carey keeps asking God for a sign, and what we see is how many signs show up that he simply refuses to see.

All we have to do is to be open to it coming to us in any possible way. It may take longer than expected, or it may not be exactly the way we think it will come to us, but what we do know is, "Ask, and we will receive"! The answer is most likely to show itself the moment that we stop thinking of how, when, or where it will come. Oh, what fun it is to see the mystery unfold around me! Whether it comes through music, meditating, dreams, Nature, or the voice of a child, friend or stranger, it is always fun to observe and see how it comes!

---

1. Marianne Williamson, A Return to Love: Reflections on the Principles of "A Course in Miracles"

That's when the world becomes a comic strip. Sometimes it is hard not to laugh at how people play out their lives, but I also have compassion for their journeys and my own because I have "been there, done that!"

Isn't one of the most important things just to have the experience? Once, when I was standing in an express line in a supermarket and the line was particularly slow because it was a small town where everyone knew everyone else and took the time to say, "How have you been, and how's the family?" I wondered, "Why did I choose this line at this time?" The man behind me started to complain, saying, "I told my wife never to send me to the supermarket, because I always get in the slowest line!" I turned around to reply.

"How often does your wife send you to the Supermarket?"

"Oh, maybe once or twice a year."

"So, you're the one who is making this line go slower then usual? This way, you can go back to your wife and say, 'I told you never to send me to the supermarket, etc.,' so she may never ask you to go again!"

I took him by surprise, and he laughed out loud, knowing full well that is exactly what he was planning to do. Then, guess what? The line began to move quickly.

In my search for enlightenment, I read books until I told myself to put them down, see if this stuff really works, and go within. I listened to speakers and had teachers, until I told myself that I had heard it all before, but in different words. Isn't it all within our own DNA, the crystallized strands that connect me to everyone, that connects me to the Universe?

The key to making proper choices is to not hurt or take advantage of anyone in the process. When this happens, new doors will open, and we will see the path more clearly and have a better idea as to what steps are needed next. If we choose inappropriately, everything gets bogged down and complicated. Choose with great integrity and personal responsibility. Be fearless and resourceful. Sometimes, some people will be hurt and feel that you have taken advantage of them because you did not meet their expectations—their picture of how they wanted you to be, but people who truly love you want you to be happy.

Plus, when you constantly give in to another's will, you enable them in their own lives and give them power over your life. That said, being in the moment is more essential than ever. The word "responsibility" simply means the ability to respond. It does not mean that if you do this or that, then this or that will happen, or that when you did this or that, this or that happened. When you are in the moment, you know from the feeling you get inside that you are making the proper choice for yourself and those around you.

To balance wisdom and folly is to trust that we have much more power and control over our life and the decisions within it than we ever realized. To be flexible, laugh, and have fun and choose what is best for us by listening to our hearts, in the moment, even if it seems the most difficult thing to do, creates harmony both now and in the future.

However the situation turns out, when you trust in your heart and use your own wisdom, you will quickly follow you inner instinct to correct the choice or move forward with it.

When I say have fun, I mean try not to take yourself so seriously! As some unknown pundit quipped, *"Blessed are we who can laugh at ourselves, for we shall never cease to be amused!"*

I had a client once who said, "How can I not take all of this serious? It is my life!"

"If you could just see how you've painted yourself into a corner," I said, "not just now, but in the past, and at the same time give yourself credit for getting yourself out of that corner by being fearless and resourceful, you would not take what is happening now, so seriously, and you would laugh at yourself."

Saying all of this, once again, does not make me any wiser then the rest of the world; it just sounds different—so maybe you can hear me.

As humans we all look alike and are created equal, but like snowflakes, we have are own uniqueness. Together we form the whole.

We look at others and see their shadows, but we neglect to see their light or we see only their light and neglect to see their shadows. We all have both. Don't kid yourself and say that you don't! It's like looking at a beautiful work of art without any shadows. It would not be as beautiful, and without both the shadows and the light, it would not be three dimensional. And are we not living in a three-dimensional world?

Epilog...Is This But a Dream?

The Unknowable informs you that here is total trust. Our truest possibilities and all our fertile dreams are held within the unknown. Relinquishing control is the ultimate challenge for the Spiritual Warrior.

A Shaman told me once that what we live here is but a dream, and that reality is on the other side.

So, is the short time that we live on Earth but a dream that we came to co-create? I've also heard that this Earth is but a learning library and that we are here to learn and return many times until we get it right. If so, there seems to be much to relearn from the history on this planet, and from the religions that have come to dominate so much of society.

Are The Ten Commandments right? These laws were written down thousands of years ago by a man who said he spoke to God, for people who were at the time doing only what they knew to do. Was it right when these laws became interpreted by others, who translated them into their own words, with their own thoughts, for their time? Was it right when Jesus, as the "Son of God," died for our sins that we did not know we committed, until someone else clarifies for us exactly what actions were and were not sins?

I cannot believe that all the billions of souls that lived before Jesus could not go to "heaven" until He came along and died for us! And I cannot believe that the Earth is the only planet in this entire universe that has living, breathing beings of God manifested upon it. Are there not billions upon billions of other planets and solar systems out there? Can't God create anything and everything? I know that all these questions have been asked thousands of times before, so why ask them again?

When I was in religion classes, my teachers tried to teach me that questioning anything taught by the church is a sin, and just considering questioning is sinful. Well, talk about being a robotic soldier! God gave each of us free will!

"Do your duty, according to what we say" is authoritarian, and "Maybe you will get your just rewards after you're dead!" doesn't seem like such a wonderful life to me.

Where's the wonder in wonderful? When I looked into other organized religions, I found that most say the same thing, but in different words. Just maybe we are here to live our journeys differently, and how are we going to do this, with so many rules made up by human beings that are just getting by themselves? I know that we have rules to avoid chaos, but isn't this world in chaos? We have rules to give us guidance, but are we that stupid that we need to be told what is right or wrong? I believe that we were given free will so we can create any experience we choose without limitations, which may either inspire ourselves and others about what to do for the betterment of the whole, or help us learn what not to do. How else is God/Spirit going to expand/evolve?

It is believed that Christ said, "Love and Be Loved." If this were the only rule and we lived by it, how much chaos would there be?

Buddha said, "Take the middle road," which sounds simple enough for me!

We honor the God(s); what about honoring the Goddess(s)? What words of wisdom did they say to our ancestors? I believe that Mary, Jesus's mother, had many words of wisdom to guide him as he grew into manhood. What about Buddha's mother and all the other Deities of the Divine Feminine? Was Eve only the disobedient wife of Adam? Wasn't she made of him? I cannot believe that the Tree of Life and the ancient symbol of healing, the snake, did not have more to say! When Eve bit into the fruit of the knowledge of good and evil, didn't she become more knowledgeable?

There was a time when women were told to obey their husbands nor were they allowed to question them. Some churches still promote this to this day, by telling women that they have to stay in a loveless, or worse, an abusive marriage. Some religions suppress women by not allowing them to drive or even show their faces.

These are simple questions that I have been asking myself and others since I was force-fed religion at an early age. When I questioned authority at the time, I was scolded, not only by my religious teachers, but also by my parents. Now we ask our government why, and we are scolded by them, telling us we are unpatriotic or immoral if we choose to not give birth, or to love whom we desire, or to even listen to new ideas. We are also told by our government that the sightings in the skies that people have seen for hundreds of years are figments of our imaginations. Are we not supposed to ask or challenge such idiocy? Must we just be led around like sheep?

I always felt that being different was a bad thing, or so I was told, and then I compromised my feelings until I was numb, but I was certainly accepted by others as 'normal.'

As a high school counselor, I told my students that being different is to be embraced, because we are here to *make* a difference. So often, I had to remind myself of what I told them, so I would not lie or compromise myself anymore. Finally and truly I became bored with trying to fit into other's people's ideas of what I should be in this life. Today very few would consider me 'normal' and that is just fine with me. I am open to embrace my full potential.

What if what Liza told me, so many years ago, is true, that I am one of many genius-creators from different galaxies and universes who are here now to create something new and different?

Could it be?

Am I?

I Am!

About the Author

Arael was born and raised by a very traditional family in a suburb of Reading, Pennsylvania. Due to the actions of her volatile parents and a few other family members, by the time she was three, she had become timid and fearful of the world around her. Not only did she experience that love was conditional within her home, but she also encountered the same ideas being ingrained into her by her traditional Roman Catholic church. There she picked up the ideas that God was to be feared and that his love was conditional, based on your behavior. At that time period, there were also few uplifting role models who could take a young, lost woman and help her see a different world.

As she matured, she began to understand intuitively that what she was being told wasn't true, but she still felt unloved. She tried to fit in, but decided that it was better to be alone and feel safe, so, for the most part, she became invisible.

Arael married young and had one child, who was the primary grace in her life. As a young mother she worked hard, multi-tasking between being a full-time housewife, with a full-time job.

After graduating from high school, she began working at Albright College in the counseling and placement center. While there, she took courses related to her job. After four years at Albright, she took another career counseling job at Reading High School because she loved being of service and wanted to work with students from all backgrounds and beliefs. Even though she still lacked a degree, she got the job because of her experience and the high recommendations from the Deans at the college.

It was at this point in her life where she began being aware of how life's gifts can be disguised in problems. For instance, during her first month at the high school, a teacher's strike gave her the opportunity to read all the resource materials and get to know all the possibilities at the Career Resource Center before she actually had to do the job.

Arael never found the time to complete her degree, but she did receive awards from Pennsylvania that recognized her accomplishments working with teachers and students to create innovative career programs.

Due to political changes in the high school that were beginning to effect her physically, she resigned. While spending a year at home, her dreams and visions began shifting her psyche and moving her into a new and very different life. Finally realizing that if she was going to be herself, she had to let go, so she sought a divorce. Her spirit guides knew that by letting go, she would then be able to study with different shamans and healers to explore who she was and what she came in to the world to do.

Today, as an independent and emotionally strong woman, she travels where she is needed and is open to what she needs to learn. She understands that no matter "how bad" life may look in the moment, everything will be good. She continues to counsel other people, only today she helps them find their true purpose in life by using her intuition, interpreting other's dreams and helping them observe what is in the now for them so they can create the future they desire.

Appendix...Runes and References

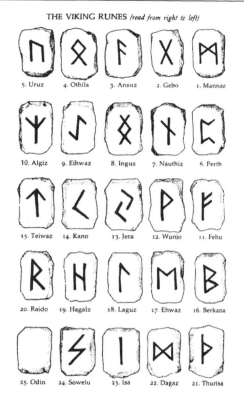

THE VIKING RUNES *(read from right to left)*

5. Uruz	4. Othila	3. Ansuz	2. Gebo	1. Mannaz
10. Algiz	9. Eihwaz	8. Inguz	7. Nauthiz	6. Perth
15. Teiwaz	14. Kano	13. Jera	12. Wunjo	11. Fehu
20. Raido	19. Hagalz	18. Laguz	17. Ehwaz	16. Berkana
25. Odin	24. Sowelu	23. Isa	22. Dagaz	21. Thurisa

from *The Book of Runes – A Handbook for the Use of an Ancient Oracle: The Viking Runes*
by Ralph H. Blum

Secret Language of Birds: A Treasury of Myths, Folklore and Inspirational True Stories Hardcover, by Adele Nozedar

Druid Animal Oracle Hardcover,
by Philip and Stephanie Carr-Gomm

Medicine Cards: The Discovery of Power Through the Ways of Animals,
by Jamie Sams and David Carson

40687340R00090

Made in the USA
Charleston, SC
14 April 2015